D1590314

SAY
SOMETHING!

SIMPLE WAYS TO MAKE YOUR SERMONS MATTER

Abingdon Press
Nashville

SAY SOMETHING!
SIMPLE WAYS TO MAKE YOUR SERMONS MATTER

This book is printed on acid-free paper.

Library of Congress Cataloging-in-Publication Data has been requested.

ISBN 978-1-5018-7439-0

19 20 21 22 23 24 25 26 27 28—10 9 8 7 6 5 4 3 2 1
MANUFACTURED IN THE UNITED STATES OF AMERICA

To Paul—God's big surprise

CONTENTS

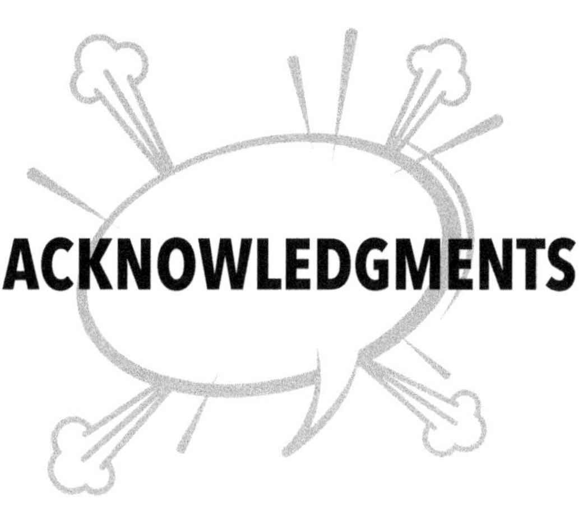

ACKNOWLEDGMENTS

I am grateful to the gifted and faithful team at Abingdon Press for making this publication possible. Specifically, I want to thank Connie Stella for her wisdom and guidance. Thanks also to Jeff Moore for creating yet another outstanding book cover. I am also grateful to Pasadena Community Church (UMC) and Johns Creek UMC for their support. They were the field in which the principles of this book were tested. Finally, I am thankful to my wife, Brandy, for her love and encouragement. Her cheers and advice spurred me on as I wrote this book.

Preface
WHY MANY CHURCHES DIE

If Protestantism ever dies with a dagger in its back, the dagger will be the Protestant sermon.

—Donald Miller, *The Way to Biblical Preaching*

If autopsies were performed on many dead churches the cause of death would be clear: pulpit failure. Nothing kills a church faster than poor preaching.

Recently Pew and Gallup did research on church growth. The results are a wakeup call to preachers. Pew's research showed that people looking for a church home value good preaching most of all.[1] Similarly, Gallup concluded that the number one reason people remain at a church is the quality of the sermons.[2] The lesson is clear: if you want to grow your church good preaching must be a top priority. While tasty coffee, cool music, and dynamic children's programs are important, if visitors don't hear inspiring sermons they will not come back to your church.

A MOMENT OF TRUTH WITH MY DOCTOR

While writing my previous book, *That'll Preach! 5 Simple Steps to Your Best Sermon Ever*, I went to see my doctor for a physical.[3] After checking my blood pressure and listening to my heart, he asked about my stress level. We both chuckled because he knows what I do for a living. Being a local pastor is always on that notorious list of most stressful vocations. I told him my stress level was high because I was trying to finish a book. "What's the book about?" he asked. "Preaching," I replied, expecting him to move quickly to a question about my diet. Instead he perked up and said, "Oh really! You mean a book on how to preach?" "That's right," I said. "It's a book to help pastors improve their preaching." His eyes widened. "Well, when it's published I want a signed copy for my pastor. If there is one thing he needs to improve it's his preaching!"

I was taken aback because I had never seen my doctor so expressive. He pushed away from his desk, leaned back in his chair, and his clinical demeanor completely disappeared. For the next several minutes he shared why his pastor's sermons were so dreadful. He told me that his church's worship attendance was dwindling because no one could bear to sit through his pastor's sermons.

I abruptly switched from patient to "homiletics professor" and asked, "Well, do his sermons lack focus? Are they difficult to follow? Is it his delivery? Do his sermons not have interesting or relevant content? Does he not explain scripture so people can understand it?" "Yes," he replied, "all of the above." Then he looked at me and said, "Don't get me wrong. I like the guy and he has done some good things for our church, but people want to connect with their pastor and hear good preaching. Folks also need the fire of faith stoked every once in a while. Do seminaries not teach preaching anymore?" I told him that seminaries do teach preaching but sometimes they leave out key components of an effective sermon. "And what are those?" he asked. I winked and said, "It's in the book." He smiled and replied, "When it comes out, make sure I get a copy." He then got back to his examination.

This conversation was an unforgettable reminder that preaching matters. If it mattered enough for a doctor to stop his examination, we as preachers better have our act together.

Every church wants a good preacher. When staff parish and pastor search committees are looking for a new pastor, what is always at the top of their list of wishes? "We want a good preacher." You never hear of a church that is content settling for a poor preacher, although unfortunately many do.

Many churches suffer because they are served by clergy who have no business being in the pulpit. Many pastors have the ability to preach but were misguided in seminary about what constitutes an effective sermon. They lecture the life out of their churches. Other pastors simply don't make preaching a priority. Instead, they spend precious time catering to the dysfunctional people in their churches.

Effective preaching is essential to the spiritual health of churches. Churches desperately need someone called by God to stand up and proclaim the gospel with skill and passion. Great preaching alone will not grow vital churches, but you can't grow vital churches without great preaching. I dare you to show me a healthy and vibrant church that does not have an effective preacher in the pulpit.

A CHURCH-GROWTH TIP THAT WORKS

Today there is much emphasis on leadership and church growth. Gurus continually pop up selling their formulas for congregational success. Some work and some don't. Many church-growth tips are not "one size fits all." But there is one church-growth tip that fits virtually every ministry context: preach well. I affirm the importance of leadership, but in our desperate search for ways to grow churches we often overlook one essential fundamental: effective preaching.

You lead from the pulpit. You are never more of a leader than when you stand before your congregation and preach well. Preaching is the one act of ministry that does the most good. In one sermon you can provide pastoral care to your entire congregation. You can cast a vision. You can motivate a large group of people to serve. You can share the gospel to several hearts so that it spreads and multiplies. When done right, one sermon can accomplish what it would take countless hours for you to do in other modes of ministry. CEOs of Fortune 500 companies would love to have the same opportunity to stand before their people once a week and remind them of the company's vision. Week in and week out preparing and delivering sermons is the best stewardship of your time. How much time are you spending on your sermons?

If more preachers spent time improving their preaching half of our problems with church growth would disappear. I dare say if I could wave a magic wand and have an effective preacher in every United Methodist pulpit, our denomination's decline would come to an abrupt halt. Within a couple of years, we might experience growth again. I believe the same is true for every mainline denomination. It is a bold statement, but I can back it up. Jesus came teaching and preaching and his sermons changed the world (Matt 9:35). It was also the sermons of the early apostles that grew the church and spread the gospel like wildfire throughout the world. If Jesus and the early apostles thought there was a better way to do ministry they would have done it.

It is clear that many sermons today are missing the mark. What is the answer? How should preachers go about delivering sermons that transform lives and grow churches? Turn the page and find out.

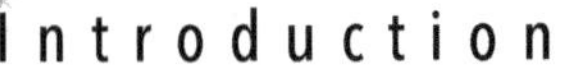

Introduction
PREACHING AS AN EVENT

A large crowd came together because they heard the noise. They were surprised because, as the apostles were speaking, everyone heard in their own language.

—Acts 2:6 ERV

A friend of mine once had lunch with the late Billy Graham. He used the opportunity to ask Graham a question about preaching. He said, "Dr. Graham, you have preached all over the world to millions of people. And when you preach you seem confident that you are preaching the very word of God. But how do you know it is really God's word and not just your own idea?" He didn't hesitate when he answered, "Oh, it is one person there, twenty people there, many people there, but when at least one person there no longer hears my voice but hears the other voice speaking."[1]

Ever experienced a sermon when you heard the other voice speaking? Ever heard a message that was so penetrating, relevant, and compelling that you no longer heard the preacher's voice but sensed God was speaking to you? This was a preaching event because you experienced the event of God in your life. Karl Barth described God as an event because God is never static. Christ reveals that God is active among us, revealing, creating, and renewing. The event of God is experienced in the preaching event.

We see the event of God on the day of Pentecost when the Holy Spirit blew on the church. Talk about an event! The Spirit spoke to each person "in their own language" (Acts 2:6 ERV). Let's not forget that a sermon was at the center of this event. Peter preached and the Holy Spirit spoke through him. The result? Thousands were added to the church that day (Acts 2:41).

I believe Pentecost is a profound reminder of what our preaching can accomplish through the power of the Holy Spirit. The result may not be as dramatic, but our preaching should "speak the language" of our listeners and create a space for God to be an event in their lives.

TWO TYPES OF PREACHING

Based on the above understanding of preaching I believe there are two types of preaching:

1. Preaching that *points* to the Event—listeners are *informed* about God and faith.

2. Preaching that *is* the Event—listeners are *transformed* by experiencing God's truth for their lives.

So much preaching falls into category 1. Preachers may be well prepared spiritually, biblically, and theologically, but their sermons never really move beyond informing people about God and the Bible. This kind of preaching is simply the sharing of information. Being informed about the faith is important, but it rarely leads to action or change.

In vital churches preaching typically falls into category 2. The sermon is an *event* for listeners. It is not just one more thing included in the order of worship or simply an opportunity to learn more about faith. Instead, the sermon is a highly anticipated event when listeners experience God's truth for their lives. This kind of preaching is relevant and connects with listeners by "speaking their language."

When a sermon is an event, preaching becomes *sacramental.* We must be careful to remember that we are vessels of God and not the source, but until we reclaim the eventful quality of preaching, souls will continue to starve and churches will continue to die.

HOW TO MAKE YOUR SERMON AN EVENT

So how do we make a sermon an event? How do we move beyond sermons that simply inform to sermons that transform? We must be "prayed up, read up, and rested up," as the old saying goes. But if prayer, study, and rest were the only requirements for eventful preaching, this book would not have been published. I know some of the hardest working and praying pastors who struggle with preaching. You can work eighty hours a week and have the prayer life of a monk and still preach terrible sermons.

What do eventful preachers do differently? They craft sermons that connect with listeners. They frame their messages in a way that fascinates, engages, and persuades. They present gospel messages that "speak the language" of those in their congregations. Simply put, eventful preachers understand that preaching is persuasive communication.

The great pulpiteer J. Wallace Hamilton said many years ago, "If people aren't interested, they're not listening."[2] I know preachers who have problems with that idea. Some even go on tirades about sermons not being "entertainment." These are often the same preachers who are killing their churches with poor preaching. Preachers can resist it, but there is no way around this truth: if people are not interested in your sermons they will not be listening. If they are not listening, they can't be transformed by your messages.

The first rule of public speaking is "know your audience." This is why every seminary should require a class in public speaking. Yes, preaching is more than giving a speech, but even preachers must use the fundamentals of public speaking and rhetoric if they want to be heard. We expect our choirs and praise bands to apply the fundamentals of music. Why should listeners not expect us to apply the fundamentals of our medium? Let's not forget that homiletics (the craft of preaching) is a healthy marriage between biblical interpretation and rhetoric (the art of persuasion).

Unfortunately, most seminaries don't require a class in public speaking. In order for preachers to learn to be effective communicators, they must join Toastmasters, wade through a myriad of books on public speaking, or spend hours on the internet watching gurus. Most preachers don't have that kind of time. That's why I have written this book. If you can spare a smidgen of time, this book can help you become an effective preacher and create sermons that matter.

This book condenses powerful communication techniques into what I call "The Essential Six Elements of Eventful Preaching." These are six nonnegotiable elements for compelling and inspiring sermons. From instruction on how to capture attention, to tips on how to tell a moving story, to keys to effective sermon delivery, this book gives you all the necessary tools to be a dynamic preacher. You can read this book quickly and immediately apply it. The "essential six" can also be your sermon stress test. Use this book to check the effectiveness of your sermon *before* you preach it. If your prepared sermon meets the essential six checklist, your sermon is going to be an event. So keep this book as a handy reference.

Turn the page and get ready to really *say something* when you preach!

The Essential Six Elements of Eventful Preaching

1. Have a Point—Will they understand it?
2. Make a Path—Will they follow it?
3. Capture and Hold Attention—Will they sit through it?
4. Make It Stick—Will they remember it?
5. Touch the Heart—Will they feel it?
6. Rehearse It—Do you know it?

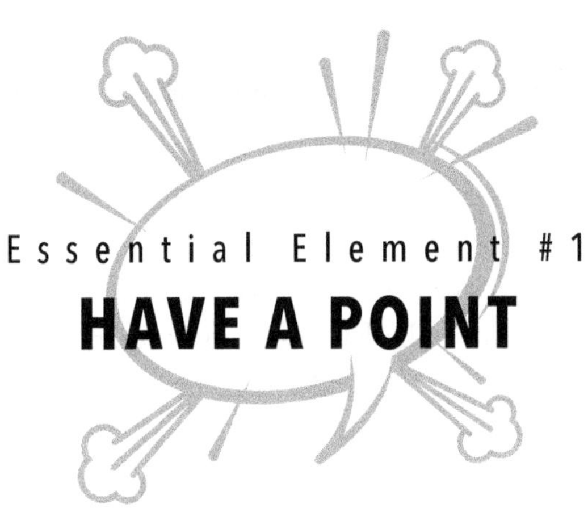

Essential Element #1
HAVE A POINT

Will they understand it?

If you aim at nothing, you will hit it every time.

—Zig Ziglar

When I took up golf I loved to hit balls on the range. It was fun to tinker with my swing and watch the ball soar in the air. Occasionally, I would take lessons. I'll never forget one of my first lessons. I set up to the ball and the kind pro stood behind me. "What's your target?" he asked. "Um, I guess to have a good golf swing." I said. He chuckled and said, "No, where are you trying to hit the ball?" I confessed that I didn't have a target. "I just thought you wanted to look at my swing." He replied, "Charley, golf is a target game. A beautiful swing without a target is useless. If you don't have a target, you can't play good golf."

It was a key lesson for me as a golfer. It is also a key lesson for any preacher. You can be the most gifted preacher in the world, but if you don't have a target it means nothing. The purpose of preaching is to get across a message, not just perform a sermon. Every sermon must have a target, a clear message or point. You should never begin preparing a sermon without knowing precisely the message you wish to convey. Unfortunately, like many golfers who mindlessly hit balls on a range, many preachers prepare sermons without a target.

Ken Untener is a priest who has taught preaching for many years. Over the years he has collected thousands of comments from people about the homilies they have heard. The number one common complaint is that homilies don't stick to one idea. One person spoke for many: "There are just too many thoughts."[1]

I am afraid the same could be said of many Protestant sermons. As a member of district and conference boards of ordained ministry in The United Methodist Church, I have heard my fair share of sermons by ministry candidates. By far the most common problem with many of the sermons is a lack of clarity. They are all over the map without a clear message. My favorite question to ask candidates during an interview is, "In one simple sentence tell me the point of your sermon." Quite often they give me a handful of sentences. It's a paragraph, not a point.

Think about the last sermon you preached. Can you sum it up in *one* simple sentence? Go ahead and try it. Is it difficult? If you cannot express your message in one clear and succinct sentence more than likely most of your congregation did not get the message.

For several years I served a church that held a sermon talkback group for high school youth. I did my best to attend each one because I knew that sermon feedback from teenagers is priceless. If you can get your message across to a sixteen-year-old (who is distracted by various things!) you can bet the rest of the congregation received the message as well. You might want to try that in your church. Be warned: high schoolers can be brutally honest.

However, if you take their feedback to heart you will become a better preacher.

TAKING DEAD AIM

When I'm preparing a sermon, my goal is to express my message in one sentence that is *clear*, *compelling*, and *memorable.*

By *clear* I mean direct and succinct. The fewer words the better. It needs to be immediately understood and repeatable.

By *compelling* I mean it needs to answer *so what?* Why should the listener care? A compelling message is one that expresses why: why the message is important to you and why it should be important to those listening. It is something you feel a great burden to share.

By *memorable* I mean when your listeners are hanging out with friends on Sunday afternoon and one of them asks, "What was the sermon about?" they can rattle off the message with ease.

Here are three examples of messages I have preached[2] that I believe were clear, compelling, and memorable:

1. Religion is reaching for God; Christianity is God reaching for us (based on John 1:14).

2. You know the Spirit is within you when you have power beyond you (based on John 15:5).

3. Sometimes the only way to the mountain top is through the valley (based on Ps 23).

As you prepare your next sermon, try whittling down your message into one sentence that is clear, compelling, and memorable. The process may take some effort, but it's worth it. Once you have that sentence, make it the gatekeeper of your message.

Don't allow anything in your sermon that does not relate to your message. This will make your sermon sharp and clear.

FROM HEAD TO HEART

The best advice I can give you about finding a sermon target that is clear, compelling, and memorable is to get out of your head and into your heart. Most preachers who fail to preach eventful sermons approach sermon preparation as only a cerebral exercise. Their noses are buried in commentaries and their minds are preoccupied with Greek syntax. This is why their sermons only inform and never transform. Don't get me wrong. Using commentaries and understanding nuances of translations are important pieces to creating a message. Preachers must do their homework in order to be faithful to the text, but that is just one small part of sermon preparation.

In order to preach eventful messages, you must prepare sermons that engage your heart, not just your head. How is this done? By putting yourself into environments that will provoke you to connect spiritually and emotionally with your upcoming sermon. Listen to your favorite music. Go for a walk. Watch people at the mall. See a movie. Meditate in a quiet garden or chapel. Do such things while prayerfully reflecting on your sermon. It sounds simple, but it's easy for preachers to compartmentalize sermon preparation to just "mind work." It is only when our hearts have been touched by our sermon that we will discover a message that will also touch the hearts of our listeners.

If you struggle to create a heartfelt message, take your preacher hat off and begin searching for a message that you need to hear. This approach will always help you find a clear, compelling, and memorable message. As the old saying goes, "A sermon is a preacher speaking loudly to himself (or herself)."

ADD CREAM TO YOUR SERMONS

It's easier for listeners to remember my sermons when I craft my message sentence into a "sticky statement."[3] I want the point of my sermon ringing in my listeners' ears as they drive away from worship. I came across a simple and powerful tool to help create sticky statements. All you have to do is add "CREAM":[4]

C—Contrast: Contrasting ideas always get our attention—good versus evil, light and dark, faith and doubt, love and hate. I used contrast when I crafted a message on Romans 8:28: "God can turn opposition into opportunity."[5]

R—Rhyme: Rhyming always aids memorization. Why do you think we still remember nursery rhymes? Andy Stanley preached a sermon about the pitfalls of comparison. His point was a nice little rhyme: "There's no win in comparison."[6]

E—Echo: Echoing is all about repetition. When a word is repeated in a sentence it often sticks. Carey Nieuwhof used the power of echo to craft this clever point: "Fixing your mind on Christ fixes your mind."[7] Here's is one of my Easter messages that echoes the words of Frederick Buechner: "The worst thing is never the last thing."[8] Another example of echo structure is: religion is reaching for God; Christianity is God reaching for us.

A—Alliteration: Preachers have been using alliteration for years. Repeating sounds always makes sentences pop. Although you can overdo it, this device can be very effective. Here's a point from Nieuwhof that uses double *b*'s: "Your boldest moments are your best moments."[9] I preached a sermon on forgiveness using alliteration. My point was forgiveness experienced leads to forgiveness expressed.

M—Metaphor: We think visually so if our listeners can see a point, they will certainly remember it. This must be why Jesus loved using metaphors when he preached. How about this one: "The eye is the lamp of the body" (Matt 6:22). Or what about, "Where your treasure is, there your heart will be also" (Matt 6:21). I used two metaphors in a sermon on Psalm 23: "Sometimes the only way to the mountain top is through the valley."[10]

Once you have a clear, compelling, and memorable point, you are ready to plan your sermon. How will you design your message for maximum impact? Continue to essential element #2.

Essential Element #2

MAKE A PATH

Will they follow it?

Listeners must sense the sermon is going somewhere fascinating or they will not take the trip.

I want to reveal the single most important idea about good preaching. If more preachers were guided by this principle, their preaching would dramatically improve. It's the same principle the late movie critic Roger Ebert used to judge every movie he reviewed: "It's not what a movie is about; it's how it's about it."[1] In the same way, it's not just what a sermon says but how it says it that counts. The way your sermon is formed or designed will determine how your listeners receive it. Never forget that listeners don't just listen to a sermon, they experience it.

An essential part of preparing eventful sermons is designing a sermon path that is appealing and easy to follow. Your sermon can have a wonderful message, but if it is not presented clearly and persuasively listeners will tune it out. Listeners must sense the sermon is going somewhere fascinating or they will not take the trip. This is why most sermons fail from faulty design, not poor content. Many preachers think only of content and don't consider the importance of sermon design. They assume listeners will be engaged regardless of how their thoughts come together. This is a mistake and only leads to frustration for your listeners.

THE "CURSE OF KNOWLEDGE"

One of the obstacles that prevent preachers from considering how they design sermons is what Harvard psychologist Steven Pinker calls the "curse of knowledge."[2] The curse of knowledge is when you forget what it's like not to know the content you are communicating. This causes a lack of empathy for listeners who don't have your frame of reference. You communicate from your level of understanding and forget that learning is a process. You tell the punchline without the setup.[3] The result: confused and uninterested listeners.

As preachers, we are often plagued with the curse of knowledge. We have been to seminary. We know the language of the church. We have a solid grasp on the Bible and theology. Yet, we forget that our listeners have not been on the same journey as us. This can lead to overwhelming listeners with information we assume they know (or want to know) and will accept. Our sermons lack the proper set up that will engage listeners and guide them to understand and receive our messages. This, more than anything else, is the cause of ineffective preaching.

In order to avoid this dreaded curse, I ask myself: What assumptions am I making about my listeners in relation to my message? Are those assumptions accurate? Do I remember what it was like before I understood my message and believed in it? How can

I create a desire in my listeners to know my message? How was I led to understand and accept this message? How can I lead listeners to understand and accept my message?

I encourage you to ask yourself the same questions. When you do, you will find yourself thinking not only of what you say but also *how* you say it. You will begin strategizing about how to design your sermon so that it captivates and convinces your listeners.

DESIGNING YOUR SERMON

How exactly do you design sermons that prevent the curse of knowledge and persuade listeners to believe in your messages? Over the years, the field of homiletics has offered several helpful sermon forms (deductive, inductive, expository, and so on). There are plenty of books that explain these various approaches. I imagine you have your own "go to" sermon structure that works for you. But have you ever considered that those who communicate well in the secular world might have something to teach us about designing sermons? I am baffled when preachers ignore the wisdom of public-speaking experts. Preaching is communicating, and if we want to do it well, we should heed the advice of specialists in the field of communication.

I have used a handful of public-speaking "formulas" or methods when designing my sermons. Not surprisingly, they have been extremely effective. We can learn a lot from traditional storytelling and expert communicators. I am going to share a few of these methods I've applied in my sermon design that have proven effective in capturing the attention of listeners.

THE BORDEN FORMULA

Richard Borden was a professor of public speaking at New York University and a noted presenter. Many years ago, he wrote a book entitled *Public Speaking as Listeners Like It.*[4] The book has become a bible for many Toastmasters and other aspiring public speakers. Borden lays out a simple but powerful four-step formula for giving speeches that captivate and convince listeners. The formula asks us to imagine our listeners are shouting each of the following four statements during our sermon or speech:

1. **"Ho hum"**

   Listeners are generally bored and complacent so don't assume they are dying to listen to you. In their mind they are saying, "Ho hum. This better be interesting." You must grab their attention at the very beginning with a provocative question, bold statement, arresting story, or some other device. Arouse your audience.

2. **"Why bring that up?"**

   Many listeners are self-absorbed, so Borden notes that we should "build a bridge" from the subject to their lives. They are thinking, "Okay, so you have my attention. What does this have to do with me? Why should I care?"

3. **"For instance"**

   Now that you have convinced your listeners to care about your topic, you must give them examples, cases, or proof to drive home your point. The listeners are thinking, "What does this look like? What examples can you give to help me understand it better? How do I know what you say is true?"

4. **"So what?"**

   When you reach the end of your presentation, you must share what you want your listeners to do with your message. They are thinking, "Now that I know this, what should I do with it?" This is when you give a call to action.[5]

It is easy to see why this simple speech formula has stood the test of time. It is also easy to see why sermons would benefit from this formula! Why not design a sermon using these four steps? Here's an outlined example of how a sermon might look using the Borden Formula:

- *"Ho hum"*: Current research shows that about half of marriages end in divorce.
- *"Why bring that up?"*: Look around the sanctuary. If current research is accurate, about half of you who are married will end up divorced. Do you want a happy, healthy marriage, or do you want to become a statistic?
- *"For instance"*: The Bible offers great wisdom about what it takes to have a happy and healthy marriage. I would like to share some of that wisdom with you today.
- *"So what?"*: Don't ever go to bed angry. Tell your spouse "I love you" at least once a day and regularly do something that makes your spouse feel special.

MONROE'S MOTIVATED SEQUENCE

Another recommended sermon development tool is Monroe's Motivated Sequence, developed by Alan Monroe, who taught public speaking at Purdue University.[6] This method is similar to the Borden Formula but focuses specifically on helping the listener solve a problem. Monroe's method follows these five steps:

1. **Attention**

   Capture your audience's attention by lifting up a struggle or problem they face. Boldly illustrate the problem with a story, quote, or statistic.

2. **Need**

   Communicate to the audience how and why this problem affects them. Show how relevant the problem is and express that it will not go away unless something is done. Use pertinent examples, research, and testimonies to convince your audience that action must be taken.

3. **Satisfaction**

   Offer a clear solution to the problem.

4. **Visualization**

   Illustrate what will happen if the solution is applied to the problem. Then illustrate what will happen if it is not applied. Use concrete examples and descriptive language.

5. **Action**

   Give listeners a clear and specific action they can take personally in order to solve the problem.

As with the Borden Formula, Monroe's Motivated Sequence is a very effective way to form a sermon, especially one that addresses a problem, mystery, or question. Here is an outlined example of a sermon utilizing Monroe's Motivated Sequence:

- *Attention*: How's your prayer life? Did you know that the overwhelming majority of active churchgoers don't have an active prayer life?
- *Need*: In my ministry I have learned from colleagues and parishioners that if you don't have an active prayer life you will not have the strength and nourishment to live out God's call for your life. I had a colleague who burned out and left the ministry because he neglected his prayer life.
- *Satisfaction*: A consistent prayer life will do wonders for you (Jas 5:16).
- *Visualization*: Imagine how in tune you will be with God and the life he has for you when you are consistently connecting with God in prayer. Imagine the confidence and the peace you will experience. If you don't commit to a regular prayer life, you might miss the movement of God in your life.
- *Action*: When you get up in the morning or before you go to sleep, spend ten minutes in prayer. Use scripture and a devotional to guide you.

THE AGAPE METHOD

In my book *That'll Preach! 5 Simple Steps to Your Best Sermon Ever,* I offer a sermon design that contains similar speech-writing elements to the Borden Formula and Monroe's Motivated Sequence. It is a useful and proven approach to preaching I call the

AGAPE method.[7] It was born out of years of preaching, teaching preaching, and an obsession to discover methods that engage and inspire. The method follows five steps using the acronym AGAPE:

A—Anticipation

Begin your message with tension by lifting up a problem, mystery, or conflict and promising to solve it. This creates anticipation in listeners. Describe your experience with the problem and how we fail at solving the problem. Express the reward that comes with finding the solution.

G—Grace

Allow God's grace through scripture to help solve the problem, mystery, or conflict. Search scripture in the hope of relieving the tension, and relate the text to the lives of your listeners.

A—Answer

Relieve the tension by communicating the answer based on scripture. Make the answer concrete. Don't just say it; show it. Use descriptive language, stories, and examples to illustrate the solution.

P—Proclamation

Move from explaining to proclaiming by expressing why your answer is important and call your listeners to act on your message. Help your listeners imagine how different their lives will be with the solution. Let your convictions fly and provide a "handle" so your listeners can grab on to your message and apply it.

E—Explosion

Create an explosion of inspiration in the hearts of your listeners with an illustration, story, video, or visual aid. Be sure to conclude the sermon soon after the explosion so listeners will feel inspired leaving worship.

Here's an outlined example of a sermon using the AGAPE method:

- *Anticipation*: Why are you a Christian? There are over forty-two hundred religions in the world. Why choose Christianity? What makes the Christian faith stand out?
- *Grace*: John 1:14 says, "And the Word became flesh . . ." (NRSV). Jesus was God's personality in human form.
- *Answer*: Religion is reaching for God; Christianity is God reaching for us.
- *Proclamation*: Imagine this world if Jesus had never been born.
- *Explosion*: The story of having our child Paul is very powerful. We thought we could never have children but he was our miracle. He has changed our lives. Before Christmas the world thought there was no hope. Then Jesus was born and he changed the world. Embrace God's embrace of you in Christ.

The reason the AGAPE method is effective is not only because it utilizes the best concepts in public speaking but also because it follows a very familiar story arc or structure. Most stories begin with a character who faces conflict (*anticipation*). This character is provided help by a special person (*grace*). The character learns a lesson or finds a solution and acts on it (*answer and proclamation*). Finally, there is a climax and/or resolution when the character defeats evil, gets back together with a loved one, or saves a village (*explosion*). Now, how many stories have you heard with the same structure? The AGAPE method follows this pattern. Why not give the AGAPE method a shot?

PREACHING FOR A VERDICT

Another powerful way to design your sermon is to prepare it like a trial lawyer.[8] A friend of mine is a former trial lawyer who now teaches at a law school. She told me that a preacher and a trial lawyer have the same goal: persuade a group of people to believe in a message and act on it. She observed that effective preachers and trial lawyers use virtually the same persuasive strategies to make their message credible and compelling.[9]

For your next sermon try seeing your listeners as a jury and use the following rhetorical strategies:

> **Promise to solve the case.**
>
> Every jury is faced with a dilemma: Is the defendant(s) innocent or guilty? Trial lawyers prepare opening statements from the jury's perspective. They realize that members of the jury have a problem to solve. Therefore, a good opening statement will validate the jury's dilemma and promise to solve it. Effective opening statements clearly and confidently express why the argument is true and convey what's at stake in the jury's decision.

The introduction of your sermon should include the same elements. An effective sermon introduction should answer the following questions: What dilemma or problem will I be addressing? What is at stake for my listeners? How will I help solve their problem, and why is it important to them? Right off the bat your sermon must validate your listeners' experience of the problem and clearly and confidently promise to solve it.

Lay out the evidence.

A jury is asked to make their decision "beyond a reasonable doubt." A jury must firmly believe an argument before deciding on a verdict. Belief always precedes action. One of the things lawyers do to bring credibility to their argument is point to evidence. There is nothing more credible than solid evidence.

Solid evidence also brings credibility to your sermon so be sure to back up your message with statistics, quotes from experts, and content from credible sources. This applies not only to apologetic sermons that defend the faith but also to any biblical message.

Dispute counterarguments.

A wise trial lawyer will anticipate questions and doubts from the jury and address them. "Some of you may be thinking, yeah but..." A wise preacher will do the same. Assume many of your listeners know all the angles to your message and can present a counterargument.

Appeal to emotions.

Good trial lawyers know that pointing to evidence is not enough. They must also appeal to the emotions of the jury. Solid evidence may influence how a jury thinks about a case, but to motivate a jury to act on what they believe (the desired verdict) a lawyer will aim for the heart.

Preachers must accept the same thing about their congregations. A reasonable and logical sermon may influence how they think, but a sermon aimed at the heart will motivate your listeners to act on your message. So, give more than logic. Stir the heart of your congregation by telling moving stories or illustrations and passionately expressing *why* your message matters.

Provide testimony.

Every lawyer knows the power of testimony. When there is personal testimony or an eye, expert, or character witness testifies it is extremely helpful to a case. The same is true for a sermon. When you give personal testimony or reference another person's testimony it is extremely effective. It is hard to argue with personal experience. Share personal stories and testimonies that have a shared context with your listeners. It gives your message more credibility and establishes a deeper connection with your congregation.

> **Call for a verdict.**
>
> In a closing argument trial lawyers will review the evidence, repeat what's at stake, and boldly ask the jury to make a decision about the case. This is their call to action or, in our language, the "altar call." Every sermon should include a bold and clear call to action. What do you want your listeners to *do* with your message? The gospel demands a response so don't end your sermon without giving your listeners the opportunity to respond to your message.

There are many effective sermon forms. These examples get you thinking more about how listeners receive your messages. Experiment with several methods and find what works best for you. When you start investing in *how* you preach as much as *what* you preach, your preaching will reach another level and listeners will be transformed by your messages.

CHECK YOUR TRANSITIONS

Regardless of the sermon form you choose, it is critical to check your transitions between major thoughts. Are your transitions smooth or abrupt? Do you connect one main thought to another, or do you assume your listeners will make that connection? What may seem like a smooth transition to you may sound to the listener like you are going down a rabbit trail.

The lack of clear and smooth transitions is usually the result of the curse of knowledge. After all, we have been living with the sermon all week. However, the congregation has not. Don't assume your listeners will naturally follow your thoughts from one movement to another. It might make perfect sense to you because you already know it, but to those who are not familiar with your text or topic, your transitions and associations might seem odd, unclear, or disjointed.

For example, do you tell an opening story and jump right into talking about the text without really explaining how the story relates to the text? You'd be surprised how many preachers are guilty of this. The listener is thinking, "Wait. What? He was just talking about his dog and now he is referring to a passage about Jesus walking on water? What?"

If you don't give your listeners an indication that you are transitioning to another movement of thought, they may lose track of your sermon. A good rule of thumb is to make at least two transitional statements between main thoughts. For example, if your sermon is on prayer, a possible transition in the sermon might be: "Do you ever struggle with prayer? Ever wonder if you are doing it right? You are not alone. *Believe it or not the disciples had questions about prayer too. They noticed Jesus habitually praying and wondered how it worked.* Let's take a look at what Jesus said to his disciples about prayer. I believe we will find some answers to our questions." The two transitional sentences are in italics. They connect the topic of prayer with the introduction of the scripture text. Listeners are now primed to hear the text.[10]

A solid sermon design is crucial for preaching engaging sermons. But there are other important communication strategies to consider if you want to capture and hold the attention of your listeners. Turn to essential element #3 and learn some trade secrets about preaching compelling sermons.

INTERLUDE

PREACHING TO MILLENNIALS[1]

Millennials (those between the ages of eighteen and thirty-four) are notoriously known to be skeptical of faith and the church. We have heard the reasons: "Millennials feel entitled and lack a sense of commitment"; "Many millennials did not grow up in the church and don't see the value in institutions like the church"; "Millennials don't feel the church does enough to address social problems"; "Millennials reject the church because of the self-righteous Christians they have known."

While I would not argue that there is some truth to these sweeping statements, there may be a simpler reason why many millennials are not in the pews: the sermon. The hard truth is that most sermons don't connect with millennials. I did some research on the millennials I know and asked them about how they listen to sermons. Based on the feedback I received there are three things a sermon must accomplish in order to reach millennials:

1. Validate their skepticism.

One of the biggest reasons why many millennials don't feel comfortable in churches is because they feel their skepticism is not welcome. Sermons that resonate with millennials validate their doubts and questions of faith. Be willing to share your own struggles with doubt and faith and what they taught you. Also, don't assume all of your listeners are Christians. Consider the possibility that there will be atheists, agnostics, and other curious people in attendance and acknowledge them in your sermon. Quite often in my sermons I will say, "Perhaps you are not a Christian and have come to worship because you are curious about Christianity. You are always welcome here." Don't underestimate the power of making such a statement in your sermon. Validate skepticism and acknowledge the curious and your sermons will go a long way for millennials.

2. Answer the "yeah, but...."

Millennials have all information in the world in their pocket. Whenever you reference a passage of scripture or use a sermon illustration they can take out their phones and Google it. In seconds they can know whether your illustration is true (or your own!) and can read other articles and sermons on your text. The result is that millennials know all the angles and can present an argument against what you are saying. The lesson: Do your homework! Consider questions and counterarguments to your sermons and answer them. "Some of you may be thinking, yeah but..." You gain a great deal of credibility with millennials when they sense you have done your research and anticipate the questions they will be asking.

3. Share why faith is important.

Millennials, more than any other generation, embrace the variety of entertainment and stimulation in our culture today. They are keenly aware of the myriad of ways they can spend their time. Therefore, sermons must not only be compelling but also convince them why investing time in matters of faith is important. Why should they have a relationship with God? Why should they read the Bible? Why should they pray? Why should they join a small group? Why should they attend worship on a regular basis? Why should they serve others? Many millennials did not grow up in church and don't know why taking a break from social media to read the Bible and pray is important. Don't assume they know why.

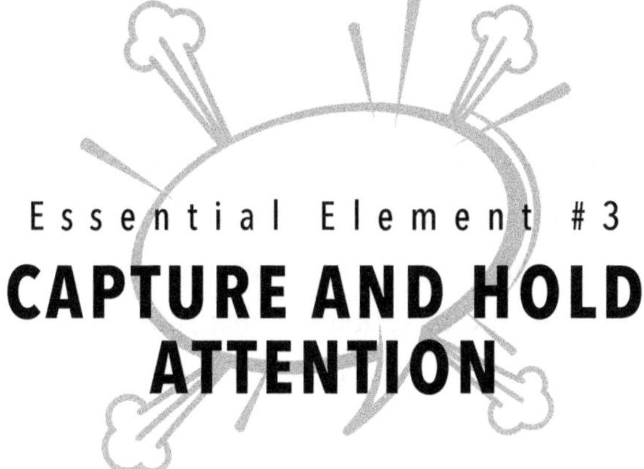

Essential Element #3
CAPTURE AND HOLD ATTENTION

Will they sit through it?

The secret to a good sermon is to have a good beginning,
a good conclusion,
and have them
as close together as possible.

—George Burns

Let's face it. It's difficult to transform listeners if our sermons don't hold their attention. They must be paying attention in order to receive the message.

I don't buy the myth that attention spans are shorter than they used to be. I believe sermons should be shorter, but not because of so-called shorter attention spans (see the interlude following this chapter). I think what we perceive as shorter attention spans is really stricter standards about what deserves our time and attention. People don't have problems paying attention to what interests them. The last movie I saw lasted almost three hours and it felt like fifteen minutes. How many of us can binge watch a Netflix series for hours on a rainy weekend? We don't struggle paying attention to what fascinates us. Therefore, if a sermon is interesting enough, listeners will pay attention.

So how do you make a sermon fascinating enough to capture and hold attention? What makes a sermon interesting and compelling? We have already established that effective sermon design is key to keeping listeners engaged. But there are other key communication strategies you must add to captivate listeners. I am going to share some trade secrets that will enable you to grab hold of your listeners and never let them go.

INSPIRE TO START A FIRE!

It is critical to capture the attention of listeners right out of the gate. There is much speculation about how much time average listeners give preachers to convince them that a sermon is worth their attention. I have heard it's anywhere from ninety seconds to two minutes. I am not sure if that is accurate, but, whatever the time, you don't have long to persuade listeners that your sermon is more interesting than their grocery lists!

The lack of time to "hook" your listeners might be an issue if you don't know the secret to capturing attention. Remember to INSPIRE your listeners from the beginning. Each letter of the word *INSPIRE* expresses a foolproof way to capture attention:

I—illustration

N—need

S—statement

P—proof

I—interaction

R—reference

E—example

I-ILLUSTRATION

The human mind is wired for illustrations and stories. As kids we begged our parents to tell us one more story at bedtime. When someone says, "Once upon a time," we are all ears. We never grow out of our love for stories, so you can never go wrong beginning your sermon with a short story, illustration, or anecdote. Your listeners will be all ears. Also using visuals aids, pictures, and videos can be helpful in telling stories and illustrating your messages. (In the next chapter I will explain more about the power of stories and how to effectively share them.)

N-NEED

How often do your sermons address a need or struggle? You will be hard pressed to find a more captivating way to begin a sermon. Many of your listeners feel beaten down by life and are hungering for a relevant message to help them overcome their problems. Right off the bat promise your listeners that your sermon will address a need or a problem they can't solve (unanswered prayer, marital conflict, fear, and so on). They will be on the edge of their seats.

S–STATEMENT

"If God created something better than sex, he must have kept it for himself!" This was a statement I used at the very beginning of a sermon I preached on sex. Believe me, it got my listeners' attention! Beginning a sermon with a bold statement never fails to arrest the attention of listeners. Just be sure to back it up with a good sermon!

P–PROOF

At the beginning of this book I referenced Pew and Gallup and their research about preaching. I imagine it persuaded you to keep reading the book! I was using the power of "proof" to get your attention. When you share eye-opening statistics, studies, interviews, or research from experts, your listeners will be eager to hear more.

I–INTERACTION

Sometimes the best strategy for capturing attention is to begin your sermon by asking your listeners to interact with others. For example, "Turn to your neighbor and say, 'Today I am going to learn something that will change my life. I am ready to hear God's word for me today.'" Listeners are usually passive participants in worship. Asking them to do something will shake things up and prime them to hear your message.

R–REFERENCE

At the beginning of the introduction of this book I shared a profound quote from the late Billy Graham. I often share that quote with preachers in seminars and workshops. Every time I do there is a palpable silence in the room. Why? Because I am sharing wisdom from someone preachers admire and respect. Why do you think companies use celebrities to sell their products? Referencing a well-known person who is admired and respected never fails to capture attention.

E–EXAMPLE

Sharing a personal example or testimony or inviting someone in the community to do the same can be a powerful way to begin a sermon. I often use this approach with stewardship sermons. I invite someone well-loved in the church to come forward and share a brief example of how giving to the church has affected them. I also share examples from my own life. Doing this makes your sermon authentic from the start, and authenticity always commands attention. Another way to use the power of example is by sharing current events or news stories. When you begin your sermon by lifting up examples in the media your message sounds fresh and relevant. Listeners pay attention to sermons that are current and in tune with the angst of culture.

INSPIRE to Flame the Fire

It's one thing to capture attention; it's quite another to keep it. The good news is that INSPIRE will help you do that too. All seven communication strategies are useful for holding attention throughout your sermon. The secret is to mix them up.

Dr. Harrison B. Summers taught radio and television broadcasting at Ohio State University. Summers's extensive research produced the secret to holding people's attention: "Give the listener something new at frequent intervals."[1]

I encourage you to keep Summers's conclusion in mind as you utilize INSPIRE in your sermons. Have you ever sensed listeners staying connected with you throughout your sermon but could not figure out what you were doing differently? Chances are it was because you presented something new at frequent intervals.[2] I am intentional about mixing up the elements of INSPIRE to keep listeners engaged. It works, so give it a shot. Tell a story, then use a metaphor or visual aid. Next, relate your text to current events and then land on a big statement or rhetorical question. You get the idea. Don't become predictable by only utilizing one strategy. The key is to bring variety to the movement of your sermon.

Emotional "Bandwidth" and Contrast

The importance of variety in preaching engaging sermons also applies to your emotional energy. If you desire to hold attention, you need to increase your emotional "bandwidth." In his book *Preaching That Moves People,* Yancey Arrington defines "emotional bandwidth" as the ability to vary your emotional tone and energy throughout a sermon.[3] Next time you watch your favorite television show or movie notice how often the emotional tone changes. This is intentional. Writers and directors know they must contrast emotions to keep listeners engaged. This is something effective communicators do as well. Like a good song or movie that takes you up high, brings you low, and then takes you up high again, a good sermon does the same. A preacher who remains at a normal emotional energy level throughout a sermon is boring. A preacher who goes low and reflects a sad or sobering energy level for the entire sermon is depressing. And a preacher who stays at a high emotional energy level is exhausting. All three levels are important and have their place, but you don't want to stay at one level too long. To be an engaging preacher you must fluctuate or contrast your emotional energy.

It follows that varying your emotional energy coincides with the content you are communicating. Communication expert Nancy Duarte believes that if you want to keep listeners engaged "contrast is key."[4] Use the power of contrast in your messages by setting opposing ideas against each other—sadness and joy, hatred and love, darkness and light, or as Duarte likes to put it, "from what is to what could be."[5]

Increasing your emotional bandwidth and using contrast might be a game changer for you. It is often the missing ingredient for preachers seeking to capture and hold attention. Simply imagine your sermon as a journey. Do you provide enough twists and turns to make it interesting for the traveler?

Now that you have a plan to capture and hold attention, you need to figure out a way for listeners to remember your message. If they can't remember your sermon, it will be left in the sanctuary. It's time to learn how to make your sermon "stick." Turn to essential element #4.

INTERLUDE

KEEP IT SHORT

I could write shorter sermons, but when I get started I'm too lazy to stop.

FOUR REASONS WHY YOUR SERMONS SHOULD BE SHORTER

I've never heard anyone say, "Our minister doesn't preach long enough." Rarely are longer sermons more effective. If you preach longer than thirty minutes your sermons are probably not as effective as you hope. In fact, keeping your sermons to about twenty minutes is optimum, but it's not always easy to do. Bishop Ken Carter of the Florida Conference of The United Methodist Church gives wise counsel to preachers: "End your sermon while your listeners are still with you."[1] There is a reason why TED Talks have an eighteen-minute rule. You don't have to say everything in one sermon. You will have another chance soon enough. Here are four convincing reasons why shorter sermons are better:

1. You will get to the point quicker.

What often frustrates listeners is when preachers take forever getting to their "why." They begin the sermon with a long joke or introduction. Listeners are thinking, "Where is the pastor going with this?" By the time they get to the point many listeners have moved to more productive things, like their grocery lists! If you shorten your sermons, you won't have time for a long introduction. You will get to the point quicker and your listeners will thank you.

2. Your sermons will be sharper.

Shorter sermons require removing unnecessary words and extraneous content. This leads to each sentence marching with a purpose. Your sermon will also have a singular target, and everything you say will point to that target. This makes for stronger sermons and easier listening.

3. Your sermons will be more memorable.

Your listeners can only absorb so much information. Therefore, the more you say, the less is heard. If you have three points, wouldn't you rather folks remember each point from three different sermons than forget them all in one?

4. You will end on time.

No one will ever complain about a sermon being too short. However, complaints about worship not ending on time is a favorite past time in church culture. If your sermons are shorter there will be less complaining. There will also be more time to sing all verses of your favorite hymn, add a song to your praise set, or have an altar call.

If you think shorter sermons mean less time in the study, think again. It takes work to make more with less. Though no one is certain who originally said it—Woodrow Wilson or Mark Twain—the saying goes: "If you want me to give you a two-hour presentation, I am ready today. If you want only a five-minute speech, it will take me two weeks to prepare." Enough said.

Essential Element #4

MAKE IT STICK

Will they remember it?

What was the sermon about?

Have you ever thought about the life span of a sermon? Some sermons die an agonizing death as they are being preached. Hopefully you haven't preached too many of those! Other sermons are decent and are discussed at lunch after worship. The good ones last beyond Sunday and people remember and apply them during the week. Great sermons are remembered for a very long time and lead to transformation. Nothing is more satisfying than when people tell you about a sermon you preached long ago that made a difference in their lives. The sermon "stuck" with them.

What if you could preach memorable sermons on a regular basis? You can! If you analyze your sermons that really stuck with people, you would discover key elements of effective communication, even if you were unaware you were applying them. I am about to show you how to apply those elements so your sermons "stick" with listeners. All you have to do is remember another simple acronym, STICK:

S—Stories

T—The power of three

I—Images

C—Concrete language

K—Key to Application

S–THE POWER OF STORIES

Let's begin with the most obvious element in sermons that stick. All good sermons contain good stories. Most of us preachers have figured out that listeners remember our stories and illustrations long after they have forgotten our clever insights and discourses. Listeners will not remember much of what we say unless it is connected to an image or story. That's just how the mind works. Knowing how to tell a good story is essential to making your sermons memorable.

Did you know there is an ironclad formula for telling good stories? Have you ever wondered why some stories fall flat and others soar? Well, it's not luck, chance, or the mood of your listeners. There is actually a method for telling good stories. Every great comedian, actor, writer, speaker, and preacher knows it. I am about to give it to you free of charge!

Let's take a look at a story I used in a sermon on the danger of pride. After reading the story I will break it down and share the magic formula. Warning: This story may cause uncontrollable laughter:

> My foursome arrived at a short par four on the back nine with a wide and forgiving fairway. I was licking my chops as I teed up the ball. I was playing with some members of my church and was determined to impress them. The smart play was to use an iron off the tee, but I wanted to show off so I pulled out my shiny new driver. I took a big swing and tagged the ball. I bombed it. Now the wind was in my favor, but I hit the ball on the sweet spot and it went a long way. In fact, I hit the ball so far that it rolled into the foursome ahead of us—a major golf "no-no." Blinded by hubris, I did not consider the proximity of the group ahead.
>
> I stood at the tee terribly embarrassed, silently rehearsing my apology speech. Up ahead I noticed a golf cart moving in my direction. It got closer and closer and closer. Soon, I realized the man driving was not going to stop! He had fire in his eyes. I quickly moved out of the way and he screeched to a halt. He got out of the cart and planted my ball in my hand. He took a hard look at me and suddenly the fire in his eyes went away. "Oh! Hi Pastor Reeb!" he exclaimed. "Great service on Sunday. Oh, and nice drive!" I replied, "Listen, I . . ." "No problem. Have a great round!" he said. And he quickly got back into his cart and drove away.
>
> I learned something valuable that day: it pays to work for Jesus! I also learned that showing off can get you into a lot of trouble. The Bible is correct. Pride does come before a fall (Prov 16:18). Or in my case before being flattened by a golf cart! My ordination is the only thing that saved me!

I've gotten a lot of mileage out of that story. I never tire of telling it. In case you are wondering, yes, it actually happened just as I described. No embellishment from this preacher! I have witnesses to prove it. Do you know why it is such a good story? Because it contains key ingredients of a good story. Communication expert Akash Karia believes all captivating stories have the "Five C's": *characters, conflict, cure, change*, and *carryout message*.[1] Great stories contain some details about the main characters. In my case it was a prideful golfer (me!) and an angry golfer. Effective stories also contain conflict. Without conflict there is no reason for folks to keep listening to your story. You must make them curious about what is going to happen next. In my story, the conflict is obvious: hitting my golf ball into a foursome and my life getting threatened by a golf cart! The cure or resolution to my story is that the angry golfer turned out to be a parishioner and he backed off. In this case the cure was a complete surprise. Listeners were not expecting it, which increased the impact of the story. Next there was a clear change in the characters of the story. Both of us were humbled! Finally, the carryout message was simple: Watch out! Pride does come before a fall.

One of the best ways to learn how to tell stories well is to watch comedians, motivational speakers, and those who deliver TED Talks. Pay attention to how they use the five C's. Notice their rhythm, timing, and ability to build tension and deliver a resolution. Many of these speakers make a killing just because they know how to effectively use the five C's That's the secret formula for good stories. Now you know!

Beyond the Five C's

If you want to dive deeper into the power of story, check out the ideas of the twentieth-century American writer Kurt Vonnegut. Vonnegut was a masterful storyteller. You can find a short video of him on YouTube explaining the shape of powerful success stories.[2] Vonnegut said that the best success stories come in three simple shapes. The first one he called "Man in a hole." In these stories someone gets into trouble and then gets out of it. The end. Now how many stories can you think of with that structure? He said the second story shape is called "Boy gets girl." These stories open with an average person on a normal day experiencing something "wonderful." As the story progresses this person almost loses wonderful. As the story comes to a close, the character gets wonderful back. Can you say Hallmark Channel?

Vonnegut said the third story shape is by far the most successful and popular in Western civilization. He said people make millions of dollars writing books and movies using this shape. Surely, we can preach memorable sermons with it! I call it "The Cinderella story" because Vonnegut used the story of Cinderella to describe its gripping progression. He said the story begins with someone dealing with circumstances at the very bottom of life, like having to live with a mean ugly step-mother and her two nasty step-sisters who did not invite her to a party. Things get a little better for the character. A fairy godmother helps her get to the party where she meets a prince. Life seems to be looking up for the character but then misfortune happens again, when she loses her glass slipper, but not without hope as before. As the story progresses, the prince finds the glass slipper and then searches for Cinderella across the kingdom. When he arrives at her home, the slipper fits perfectly and she marries the prince and experiences "off-the-scale" happiness.

Having knowledge of these three story shapes can help you choose memorable stories for your sermons. However, keep in mind that your stories do not always have to have a happy or funny ending. As preachers, we know some of the most effective stories are those that contain powerful lessons through sad, moving, or sobering resolutions. Think of the parable of the prodigal son. The real resolution of that story is not the prodigal's homecoming; it is the resentful elder son standing outside the party deciding whether or not to go in. Did he ever go in? We don't know. I believe Jesus wanted us to ask, "If I were in his shoes would I go in?"

Finding Good STORIES

So where do we find the best stories for sermons? In everyday life! Now, that's a shocker, isn't it? The best stories for sermons are found by simply paying attention to your life and the lives of those around you. Have you ever heard the comedic routines of Jerry Seinfeld or Brian Regan? They make a great living just by observing life and telling people about it. Watch one of their routines and write down what they talk about—kids, school, restaurants, people in airports, grocery stores, shopping malls, food, weddings, marriage, playing a round of golf, sitting in traffic, going to the doctor, sitting through a boring dinner party, and so on. Now we can all relate to most if not every one of those experiences. When you tell stories about everyday life, listeners find it easy to connect with you.

Great stories and illustrations are everywhere. They are in movies, books, shopping malls, amusement parks, waiting rooms, park benches, concerts, ball games, hospitals, the people sitting next to you in traffic, in your dog or cat, and in the crazy and wise things children say. Listen to children. They are a tremendous source of sermon material. In fact, just listen to people in general. Conversations and interactions with people can be a profound well for sermon content.

We as preachers sometimes struggle finding good sermon material because we wear so many different hats and compartmentalize our roles. When we are doing tasks that don't directly correspond to preparing sermons we forget to see the plethora of sermon material around us. Always be on the prowl for sermon ideas and material. It is helpful to develop the discipline of being a collector of sermon ideas and content. Always have your phone or pen and pad handy. When you see something useful, immediately write it down so you don't forget it.

T–THE POWER OF THREE

How many jokes have you heard that begin like this: "Did you hear the one about the rabbi, the priest, and the minister . . ."? What about, "There were three men sitting at a bar . . ."? Or how about this one, "A Baptist, a Catholic, and a United Methodist run into each other at a liquor store . . ."?

As a kid, how many times did you hear about *The Three Musketeers*, *The Three Little Pigs*, or *Goldilocks and the Three Bears*?

At Christmas time how often do you watch *A Christmas Carol* and observe Scrooge getting a chance at redemption by learning lessons from the ghosts of Christmas *past*, *present*, and *future*?

Are you noticing a pattern here? It is called "the power of three" and it is an extremely effective communication principle. It has been proven over and over again in all forms of communication that when things come in threes they are more satisfying and memorable. Putting together three items is often catchy because rhythm and brevity is combined to establish a pattern with a small amount of information.[3]

Savvy advertisers use the power of three all the time: "The Few. The Proud. The Marines"; "Stop, Look, and Listen" (public road safety slogan); "Play, Laugh, Grow" (ad for Fisher-Price).

Or, consider the public service mantra "Stop, drop, and roll" about what to do in the event you wake up to a house fire.

Many churches use the power of three as part of their mission and vision statements. My church's slogan is "Connect, Grow, Serve." Even in a court of law the power of three is used when a witness is asked, "to tell the truth, the whole truth, and nothing but the truth." And speaking of truth, Jesus used the power of three when he described himself as "the way, the truth, and the life." Of course, we know that "the power of three" is biblically and theologically sound. After all, we do pray to the "Father, Son, and Holy Spirit"!

Surprise!

The effectiveness of the power of three is felt not only in its combination of rhythm and brevity but also in the way it can create surprise or bolster emphasis of a word or idea. This is done by establishing a contrast between the first two elements and the third. For example, a joke's punch line or surprise is often experienced with the description of the third character. This is known as a *comic triple*:

> A Baptist, a Catholic, and a United Methodist die and go to heaven. Saint Peter doesn't have their rooms ready so he asks Satan to hold them for a few hours. Satan calls Peter and says, "You have to come get these guys. The Baptist is saving everybody. The Catholic is forgiving everybody. And the United Methodist has already raised enough money for air conditioning!"

The surprise and laugh occur by singling out the United Methodist and placing him last in this old joke.

Not only do we see this effect used in jokes and comedy, but also it is used in dramatic stories, a *dramatic triple*, if you will. In fact, Jesus used it when he taught and preached. Remember the parable of the talents? There were three characters in that story: a man with five talents, another with two, and another with one. The third character with one talent was singled out as being unfaithful (Matt 25:14-30). What about when Jesus was accused of eating with sinners and tax collectors in Luke 15? He responded by telling three stories: the parable of the lost sheep, of the lost coin, and of the lost son. Jesus and the writer of Luke saved the most dramatic parable for last. I don't believe this was an accident.

"Abide These Three"

So how do we use the power of three to make our sermons memorable? Clearly, we should consider the power of three when planning to tell stories or jokes in our messages. Another obvious way to use the power of three is by preaching sermons with three points. Although there are many effective ways to form your sermons (see essential element #2), there is a reason why three-point sermons have stood the test of time.

We can also use the power of three when constructing sentences and phrases. For example, let's take one of the most memorable chapters in the Bible, 1 Corinthians 13. When Paul wrote these inspiring words, he knew they were going to be read aloud so he applied the power of three throughout the chapter. Why do you think this text is so popular? Yes, it is about love, but it is not just the content that makes it so beautiful. It is also the rhythmical way repetition and the power of three come together. Notice how

Paul combines three phrases in verse eight: "But as for prophecies, they will come to an end; as for tongues, they will cease; as for knowledge, it will come to an end" (NRSV).

In verse eleven, Paul repeats the phrase "like a child" three times: "When I was a child, I spoke *like a child*, I thought *like a child*, I reasoned *like a child*" (NRSV, emphasis added).

Notice how Paul combines the power of three with repetition at the beginning of the chapter by repeating the refrain "but do not have love" three times:

> If I speak in the tongues of mortals and of angels, *but do not have love*, I am a noisy gong or a clanging cymbal. And if I have prophetic powers, and understand all mysteries and all knowledge, and if I have all faith, so as to remove mountains, *but do not have love*, I am nothing. If I give away all my possessions, and if I hand over my body so that I may boast, *but do not have love*, I gain nothing. (vv. 1-3 NRSV, emphasis added)

Paul ends the chapter using the power of three by combining three key ideas and placing love in the prominent third and last position: "And now faith, hope, and love abide, these three; and the greatest of these is love" (v. 13 NRSV).

Perhaps Paul's most recognizable use of the power of three is found in 2 Timothy 4:7: "I have fought the good fight, I have finished the race, I have kept the faith" (NRSV).

The Last Word

First Corinthians 13 and 2 Timothy 4:7 not only demonstrate Paul's use of repetition and the power of three but also teaches us to be intentional about which words end our sentences.

The last word or phrase spoken in a sentence carries more weight for the listener. When you are constructing your sentences and phrases consider which idea is the most important or the one you want to emphasize the most. Just like good stories often single out the third or last element for emphasis, key sentences and phrases should end with the most important word or idea. Imagine if Paul had written these words to Timothy instead: "I have fought well. My race is over. My faith is strong." It does not have the same punch or emphasis, does it? Paul knew the power of a spoken sentence is felt in the last word.

Consider the beloved patriotic phrase "In God We Trust." Notice how the tone and message of the phrase changes when we *say* it this way: "We Trust in *God*." When God is placed last in the sentence its complexion is transformed. It is more appropriate because God does indeed have the last word!

Repetition, Anaphora, Ellipsis, Oh My!

It is important not to overdo the power of three or any other rhetorical device. Not every sentence or phrase in a sermon should use the power of three. Your sermon would sound like a Dr. Seuss story. Simply remember the power of three when you are putting together thoughts, sentences, and phrases that you want to emphasize. And don't obsess about the last word of every single sentence in your sermon. That is a waste of time, and you will drive yourself crazy. Again, when you come to places in your sermon that require emphasis consider the best way to end your sentences.

Scores of books have been written on the power of three, repetition, and other rhetorical techniques like alliteration, ellipsis, asyndeton, anaphora, balance, and hyperbole. I encourage you to look up such concepts. Using rhetorical devices seems like a lost art but they will never go out of style. They are still very effective when seeking to make your sermons persuasive and memorable.

I–IMAGERY

It has already been made clear that the mind thinks visually; therefore, using images and descriptive language is essential to make your sermons stick. In this way the minds works like Velcro. The rough side of Velcro is made up of tiny flexible hooks and the soft side is made up of small soft loops. When you put them together the hooks latch on to the loops. That's what makes Velcro stick. Imagine the mind as a bunch of tiny flexible hooks eager to hook to an idea. Now think of stories, images, and illustrations as small soft loops the mind connects with that makes the idea clear, concrete and memorable. An idea associated with an image "sticks" to our minds like Velcro.[4]

A pastor once used a powerful visual aid to make his sermon stick. He invited a man to come up on the platform and handed him a glass of water. As the pastor preached, he bumped the man's arm and water spilled on the pastor. The pastor turned to the man and asked, "Why did you spill water on me?"

The man replied, "Because you bumped me."

"I know I bumped you. But why did you spill water on me?"

"Uh... I spilled water on you because you bumped my arm."

"Let me put it this way: Why did you spill water on me? Why didn't you spill coffee? Or lemonade? Or tomato juice?"

"Because that's what was in the glass—just water."

The pastor turned to his listeners and said that every day we fill ourselves with good character choices or bad character choices. Inevitably, life is going to bump us around and provoke what is inside of us to spill out. What will come out? Courage or cowardice? Forgiveness or resentment? Selfishness or self-control?[5] Now that message sticks, doesn't it?

I used a powerful image in a sermon to describe critical decisions in life. I got the idea from a sermon by King Duncan.[6] My text was Deuteronomy 30:19, when Moses said to the people of Israel, "I have set before you life and death.... Choose life so that you and your descendants may live" (NRSV). I expressed how some decisions in life are crossroad decisions at which we can choose life or death. Do we choose to follow idols or follow the living God? Do we give in to temptation or do the right thing? To help drive home this point I showed a picture of "Dante's View" in Death Valley. From Dante's View you can see the lowest spot in the United States, called Black Water. It is a depression in the earth two hundred feet below sea level. But from Dante's View you can also see Mt. Whitney, which is the highest peak in the United States at 14,500 feet. I said that sometimes our life choices are like Dante's View. We can choose the high road to life or the low road to death.

C–CONCRETE LANGUAGE

Sermons often deal in abstract concepts. The problem is most listeners will not remember an abstract idea. In order to make our sermons memorable we must put flesh and blood on our ideas by using concrete language. Linguist Samuel Hayakawa came up with a valuable tool to help communicators express concrete ideas. It is called "the Ladder of Abstraction."[7] At the top of the ladder are big, *abstract* ideas like faith, hope, and love. At the bottom of the ladder are *concrete* ideas like praying hands (faith), a new born baby (hope), or the cross (love). Like a real ladder, the bottom of the ladder of abstraction is best supported by what is solid or concrete—tangible words and specific descriptions. As you go up the ladder, ideas get more general and abstract.[8] In order to be an effective communicator, you must move up and down the ladder.

Hayakawa's Ladder of Abstraction can be a helpful tool for preachers. Preachers are usually skilled at describing abstract concepts or the "big ideas" such as faith, love, hope. What many preachers struggle with is giving specific, concrete examples of these big words. It is only by giving specific examples of your sermon's big picture that it becomes inspiring and memorable.

Here is an excerpt of a sermon I preached entitled, "Dying to Live."[9] It was based on Jesus's words, "For those who want to save their life will lose it" (Matt 16:25 NRSV). Notice that I began with the abstract idea of dying to live and then made it more concrete by giving specific examples:

> All of us must die in order to give birth to something new. A bad habit must die to provide room for a good one. Certain ways of thinking must change in order to get the desired action. A place of comfort must be left in order to move to a healthier one. All such radical changes must occur in order for something new to be born.
>
> Just listen to newborns scream as they make their miraculous move from the familiar womb into a foreign world. It must be awful for them, but there is no other way for birth to happen.
>
> Ask a recent graduate how difficult it is to leave college and enter a new world of responsibility. Such change is tough, but without making that leap there is no opportunity, growth, or accomplishment.

> Ask a couple how challenging it is to let go of their own pursuits in order to raise a child. A big sacrifice, but there is no greater joy than raising a child.
>
> We must die in order to live. We must be broken in order to be made whole. We must give in order to receive.

Here is another example of a sermon I preached using a concrete illustration to describe the work of the Holy Spirit:

> We need to reaffirm our belief in the Holy Spirit. It lives inside every Christian. The Holy Spirit is willing to nourish, guide, and empower us for living. Do we realize how fortunate we are to have the Holy Spirit mentoring us?
>
> Let's say for a moment that I went into a music shop and bought a guitar. After I bought the guitar I signed up for group lessons. Imagine if Eric Clapton walked into one of my lessons and said to me, "I like the way you play. I see some potential in you. I am going to give you this option. You can continue taking this class once a week, or I will meet with you one on one for an hour every day and teach you everything I know."
>
> What do you think I would do? I would go crazy, "Yes! Yes! When do we start?" Maybe a year later someone would ask me, "Where did you learn how to play the guitar? Who taught you?" Perhaps I would be modest and say, "I just took some lessons." They would reply, "No, you did not take lessons. You were taught by a master. You can really play!"
>
> In the same way when we allow the Holy Spirit to mentor us through regular prayer and scripture reading it won't be long before someone asks, "Where did you get that insight?" or says, "There is something different about you." You might reply, "I go to church once a week." And they will respond, "No, you don't just go to church once a week. You have been spending time with the Holy Spirit."[10]

When you are preparing a sermon, always ask yourself, "How can I make my ideas concrete, tangible, and specific? What is the best way to make this idea come alive for my listeners?"

K–THE KEY TO APPLICATION

Listeners will remember your message if they are given a tangible way to live it out; so hand them a key to help them apply the sermon. A sermon is meant to be lived, not just heard. This is why every sermon needs a handle the listener can take into their own hands. Provide a "call to action." Is your sermon about prayer? Give them a simple daily prayer plan. Does your sermon address poverty? Ask your listeners to volunteer at the food bank. Preaching on evangelism? Encourage each member of your congregation to bring a friend to worship the following Sunday. Again, how can your listeners apply your message? A sermon that can't be applied is left in the sanctuary and forgotten.[11]

Now that you have plans to make your sermon STICK, you need to consider another essential element to eventful preaching. I call it the "secret sauce" of compelling sermons. Turn to essential element #5 to learn more.

Essential Element #5

TOUCH THE HEART

Will they feel it?

People will forget what you said. People will forget what you did. But people will never forget how you made them feel.

—Maya Angelou

Aristotle said three things are essential to persuade: ethos, which is an appeal to ethics by convincing listeners of your credibility; logos, which is using logic and reason to persuade; and pathos, which is motivating your listeners by creating an emotional response.

I believe Aristotle was correct, but I don't believe logic and emotion are equal when it comes to persuasion. Why? "Emotion leads to action while reason leads to conclusions."[1] Well-read and studied sermons will stimulate the mind, but if you don't engage the heart your listeners will not act on your message. You might impress your listeners with your intellect and education, but you won't find many pledge cards in the offering plate or people coming down the aisle. Your listeners must feel before they want to know and do.

FIND YOUR "WHY?"

So how do you engage the hearts of your listeners? One critical way is by expressing why the message is important to you. Listeners are not moved by your knowledge or clever insights; they are moved by why you believe the message is important. Sharing your "why" is the secret sauce of good preaching because a convicted preacher is a compelling preacher. The world is hungering for genuine expressions of truth. Your listeners will be motivated to act on your message when you express what motivates you to preach the sermon. People want you to speak from your heart to their heart. When you get in touch with that, you will find the sweet spot of preaching.

GET PERSONAL

Another way to touch the hearts of your listeners is by sharing personal experiences that have a common context. When listeners can personally relate to stories and events in your life they feel a deeper connection with you and your message. The trick is recalling the appropriate personal stories. The right stories are in your memory bank. All you have to do is tease them out. In his book *Steal the Show*, communication expert Michael Port teaches a simple trick to remembering personal stories.[2] Next time you are preparing a sermon and need a good personal illustration or story just use the following prompts Port recommends:

1. **People**

   Think of all the significant people in your life. Go all the way back to your childhood and then back to the present day. Think of parents, grandparents, teachers, girlfriends, boyfriends, cousins, aunts, uncles, neighbors, friends, enemies, business partners, coworkers, repair men, waiters, waitresses, coaches, and so on. Thinking of the people in our lives will often trigger memories of useful personal events and stories.

2. **Places**

   Think about vacations you have taken, special places you have visited with loved ones, mountains you have hiked, sports stadiums you have visited, houses you have lived in, playgrounds, high school and college campuses, pools, lake houses, ski resorts, swanky hotels, gross hotels, hospitals, doctor's offices, beaches, golf courses, tennis courts, holy sites, and churches. Special places have a way of jogging our memory of significant personal experiences.

3. **Things**

   Think of the first album you owned, an autographed baseball, your first car, your worst car, pets, jewelry, hand-me-down clothes, boats, golf clubs, tennis racket, china, treadmills, dining room table, recliner, comfy sofa, beds, fishing rods, Christmas trees, Christmas tree ornaments, computer, cell phone, iPad, and so on.

4. **Times and Events**

   Reflect on the birth of your first child, your first day of middle school, first day of high school, weddings, anniversaries, baptisms, confirmation, first sermon you preached, first church you served, Thanksgiving, Christmas morning, graduations, first kiss, first date, worst dates, breakups, deaths of loved ones, and funerals.

If you use these prompts or triggers, you are almost guaranteed to remember a personal story that will be useful for a sermon. Remember that the most effective personal stories have a shared context with your listeners. For example: sibling stories, stories about Christmas mornings, losing loved ones, first days of school, fights with best friends, watching football games, being embarrassed by your parents as a kid, and so on.

Sharing personal stories and experiences in your sermon can be powerful, but be careful not to overdo it. If listeners feel like your sermons are always about you, they will be turned off. A well-placed personal example can be extremely useful, but practice moderation.

Use humor.

I imagine when you read the previous prompters, you remembered some humorous events in your life. Humor is a very powerful preaching tool. It can smuggle your message into the hearts of your listeners. When people laugh their defenses are down. They are relaxed, engaged and open to your sermon. There is much truth in the advice often attributed to novelist Charles Dickens: "Make them think, make them laugh, make them cry." Although you don't want to manipulate listeners, you do want to move them emotionally, and humor is often the best way to their hearts.

You may be surprised to discover that Jesus used humor when he taught and preached. For example, Jesus used humor when he compared a fault finder to a man with a log in his eye telling another man to get the speck of wood out of his eye (Matt 7:3). You can imagine Jesus's listeners chuckling over that one. How about Jesus comparing the religious legalists of his day to a man who polished the outside of his drinking cup but forgot to clean the inside (Matt 23:25) or a man picking a gnat out of his drink and then swallowing a camel (Matt 23:24)? Or what about when Jesus compared a rich man entering the kingdom of heaven to a camel trying to squeeze through the eye of a needle (Mark 10:25)? Jesus often used humor through exaggeration, irony, and paradox. If you see these teachings of Jesus as comic strips it is apparent his intention was to make his listeners laugh as they absorbed his lesson. Jesus knew the value of humor in engaging his listeners with his message.[3]

So how do you use humor effectively in a sermon? In addition to sharing humorous personal stories, there are simple strategies to make listeners laugh. Here are four effective ways to bring humor into your sermons:

Surprise them!

The common element in all humor is surprise. We laugh when something surprises us. One of the easiest ways to make listeners laugh through surprise is to "create an expectation and then suddenly break it."[4] I surprised my congregation by making this statement in a farewell sermon: "Did you see the preacher in the news who asked his congregation for 75 million dollars to buy a jet? Crazy, huh? Of course, if any of you are looking for parting gift ideas for me, that would be a good one. I promise to put the name of the church on it!" (laughter).

My congregation was expecting me to give some critical commentary about the preacher asking for a jet (which I did later in the message!). Instead, I surprised them by joking about how it would make a wonderful parting gift.

In his TED Talk, Daniel Pink surprises his listeners by making this observation about his experience as a law student: "I didn't do very well. I, in fact, graduated from the part of my law school class that made the 90 percent... possible" (laughter).[5]

Dan's "setup" was creating the expectation that he graduated at the top of his class. When he broke in with the word *possible* he shattered that expectation and surprised listeners by sharing that he really graduated at the bottom of his class. This sudden surprise is what got the laugh. The other reason this line is funny is because Dan was using the oldest trick in the book of humor: making fun of himself, also known as self-deprecating humor.

Use self-deprecating humor.

Making yourself the butt of your jokes never fails. When you're willing to poke fun of yourself you appear humble and on the same level as your listeners. You also come across as a fun-loving person who doesn't take yourself too seriously. This always endears you to listeners. What's more is that if you're willing to poke fun at yourself you will always have good material!

In the same TED Talk Daniel Pink made the following statement: "I never practiced law a day in my life. I pretty much wasn't allowed to" (laughter).[6]

Here's another example of self-deprecating humor. I once got up to preach after a liturgical dance routine and said: "I want to thank the dancers this morning. It went exactly as we practiced it" (laughter). Anyone who knows me knows that liturgical dance is not one of my specialties!

Exaggerate.

Exaggerating is a form of surprise that often gets laughs. I once got up in the middle of a Christmas concert to take up an offering and said to the big crowd: "Thank you for coming tonight. Now we are going to take up the first of six offerings for our music ministry" (laughter).

The idea of taking six offerings got a big laugh because it was a huge exaggeration, although who among us would not like to take up six offerings?

Another example of exaggeration comes from Ken Robinson's TED Talk. In his presentation Ken spoke of his multitasking wife: "If she's cooking, you know, she's dealing with people on the phone, she's talking to the kids, she's painting the ceiling, she's doing open heart surgery over here" (laughter).[7]

Be honest.

Sometimes the easiest way to make listeners laugh is simply by being candid. When you speak the truth about something other people are reluctant to express, it often comes across as humorous. You are naming what annoys or bothers people, and listeners laugh as if to say, "Yes, I feel the same way!" Obviously, you must use discretion about your level of honesty, but making frank observations about life and faith can make your listeners roar with laughter.

Bishop Sue Haupert-Johnson got a big laugh when she made this observation during a sermon: "We know a lot of people who read the Bible every day and are still jerks!"[8] Very true, and very funny.

There are many other ways to be humorous, but I have found these four approaches to be effective. Obviously, telling jokes is another way to make people laugh, but be careful which jokes you choose. Some are so corny you may get groans rather than laughs. Others are simply inappropriate for a sermon. If you find a good joke, by all means use it, but stretch your ability to be humorous by using surprise, self-deprecation, exaggeration or hyperbole, and honesty in your sermons.

Finish strong with a mic drop.

I have a friend who loves to entertain. If she is unsure about a meal she has prepared, she offers a mouth-watering dessert. This way, if the meal is less than stellar it won't matter. The delicious dessert will be the first thing remembered and her guests will conclude it was a wonderful evening. Preachers would be wise to remember this when preparing sermons. If you are unsure about the effectiveness of your sermon, just finish strong and your listeners will likely walk away from worship appreciating the sermon. The strong conclusion is what they will remember most. This is the *law of recency* at work. The last thing experienced is the first thing remembered.

A helpful guide to finishing your sermon strong is remembering the acronym CLOSE. Each of these can be an effective way to close your sermon. You can also combine them when appropriate:

> **C—Circle Back:** Refer back to a powerful quote, illustration, or story that opened your sermon.
>
> **L—Lead them to Christ:** You can never go wrong concluding your message asking listeners to affirm or reaffirm their faith in Christ.
>
> **O—Opportunity:** Give your listeners an opportunity to respond to your message with a call to action (turn in pledge cards, sign up for a ministry, come to the altar, and so on).
>
> **S—Summarize:** Review your main idea or key points and remind listeners what's at stake.
>
> **E—Explosion:** Close with an explosion of inspiration by sharing a moving story, illustration, or example.

After your sermon has a compelling point, a fascinating path, a strategy to be captivating and memorable, and a plan to touch hearts, you are ready for essential element #6.

INTERLUDE

PREACH LIKE TED

TED Talks are watched 1.2 billion times a year![1] Whenever someone tries to tell me that preaching is an outdated medium, I give them that statistic. TED Talks are not sermons, but they are public addresses; and their staggering popularity reveals that the public still hungers for people to speak passionately about an idea. If a sermon is anything it is an inspired speech about the one who had the first idea.

If you are not familiar with TED, it is a nonprofit organization dedicated to spreading ideas through short, powerful "talks." These videos saturate the Internet and the topics range from science to psychology to global issues. If you are familiar with TED, I imagine you have your favorite "talks," and you have watched them more than once!

In my preaching seminars I encourage preachers to watch TED Talks to learn how to be better communicators. Since we have been called by God to communicate the most transforming message in history, we must continually work at honing our craft. I can't think of a better way to do that than to learn why TED Talks are so insanely popular.

WHY ARE TED TALKS SO POPULAR?

Why have over a billion people worldwide viewed these eighteen-minute speeches? Communication expert Carmine Gallo believes

he has cracked the code. In his book *Talk Like TED*,
three fundamental reasons why most TED Talks are s
They are "emotional, novel and memorable."[2] They
hearts, teach us something new, and present ideas in unforgettable ways. Now think of the best sermons you have heard. I'm willing to bet they were also "emotional, novel and memorable." This is the great *triumvirate* of all public speaking. Here's why:

1. Emotional

The only way you will persuade listeners to learn and act is if you move them emotionally. Now I know we as preachers must always be careful not to be manipulative, but let's get real. Listeners are not motivated to do anything unless their hearts have been touched.

Application: You must be passionate about your sermon and that passion must come through in your delivery. You must also communicate ideas, stories, and illustrations that not only stimulate the mind but also touch the heart.

2. Novel

Obviously not every sermon is going to present a new idea. We have over two thousand years of preaching tradition! Sometimes the best sermons are those that remind us what we already know in novel ways. I believe this is why preachers like Barbara Brown Taylor and the late Fred Craddock are so popular. Most of their sermons do not express new ideas about the gospel; they communicate familiar ideas in unique ways.

Application: Try new sermon forms and structures. Do you always preach sermons with three points? Try preaching a sermon with only one point. Do you always communicate your main idea at the beginning of your sermon? Try preaching inductively and reveal your main idea at the conclusion of your sermon. Do you always end with a story? Try concluding your sermon with a video or skit. What metaphors, stories, or images can you use that will make your message come alive? Read and watch other preachers noting the approach and structure of their sermon.

3. Memorable

I recognize that if you are an "every Sunday preacher" like me, it is very difficult to do something memorable every Sunday. After all, TED presenters only have one speech to give! We have to come up with a new sermon every week! We can't do stunts every week. We will be stuck with the impossible task of trying to top ourselves with every sermon. However, doing something memorable doesn't always mean a stunt. Try sharing a personal testimony, using a visual aid, interviewing someone, including a song in your sermon, or giving your congregation an item that will remind them of the message. Big stunts work too but use those sparingly. I once heard of a preacher who had someone playing the role of Jesus interrupt his sermon. That's memorable, but you can't do those kinds of stunts every week.

Application: Get a team of creative people together and hand them a list of your upcoming sermons. Invite them to think of creative and memorable ways to present the messages. Some preachers use their worship team for this purpose. Others ask particular members of the congregation to participate.

Essential Element #6

REHEARSE IT

Do you know it?

The more I practice the luckier I get.

—Jerry Barber

I remember watching a fascinating TED Talk by June Cohen, the executive producer of TED Media. Her presentation was entitled, "What Makes a Great TED Talk?" It is Cohen's job to pick and prepare TED speakers. In her experience preparing a myriad of speakers and listening to hundreds of talks she said the most important element to a successful TED Talk is *practice.* That's right. Cohen believes the biggest difference between a successful TED Talk and one that falls short is whether or not the speaker spent time practicing the speech.[1]

Cohen's conclusion may seem like common sense, but is it so common? Do you rehearse your sermons? I don't mean going over it in your head. I mean literally preaching your sermons out loud. If you don't you are probably not preaching to the best of your ability. After all, we tell kids that if they want to improve at playing the piano or throwing a baseball they must practice. The same is true of preaching.

I know some preachers who are not comfortable with the idea of practicing or rehearsing sermons. They think their sermons will sound contrived or they are not leaving room for the Holy Spirit to work. My usual response to them is, "Is the Holy Spirit not active in your study too?" Praise bands and choirs feel the need to rehearse and we don't criticize them for it. In fact, we would be upset if they didn't! Are preachers exempt from the need to practice? Absolutely not.

I never go into the pulpit without having practiced my sermon several times. I have found that rehearsing my sermons gives me more freedom in the pulpit. I never feel lost or afraid of forgetting my ideas. There is a well-worn sermon path in my brain that allows me to deviate from my path when led and still find my way back home. Rehearsing my sermon out loud also sparks new ideas that didn't come to me when I was preparing it. Conversely, when I hear myself preaching the sermon I discover that what looked good on paper does not sound so good when spoken. I am able to make key adjustments.

I know practicing your sermons takes extra time and effort but it's worth it. Start getting up earlier on Sunday mornings (or whenever you go over your message) to rehearse your sermons. You will be amazed how much more effective you are in the pulpit. The more effective you are in the pulpit the more people will show up for worship. Right or wrong that's the way church life works. Remember, as Olympic swimmer Michael Phelps once said, "If you want to be the best, you have to do things that other people aren't willing to do."

KEYS TO EFFECTIVE SERMON PREPARATION AND DELIVERY

As you prepare and practice your messages, it is important to remember that a sermon is an oral event. It is meant to be heard, not read. Many preachers struggle with preaching because they prepare sermons like an essay or term paper, which are written for the eye. It may read well, but it falls flat when preached. A sermon written on paper is worlds apart from a sermon that is delivered. If you prepare a sermon manuscript, be sure you are writing for the ear, not the eye. Your sentences need to be shorter, active, and descriptive, and your phrasing and rhetoric should reflect a sense of timing.

To help you prepare sermons for the ear I suggest preaching your sermon "out loud" the moment you begin preparing it. Say it as you write it and write it as you say it. This will guarantee your sermon is prepared for the ear. Later, when you are rehearsing your completed sermon, you will hear and feel the difference. Your sermon will have the flow of oral language. You won't have to twist, turn, and manipulate your sentences to sound good. Your words will be easier to say and hear. If you prepare an outline instead of a manuscript, the same routine applies. Preach your outline into existence. Your notes will trigger the appropriate words, phrasing, and rhetoric for effective delivery.

Learning how to effectively deliver your sermons is another benefit to preparing "out loud" and rehearsing. It is easy to become so preoccupied with the content of our sermons that we neglect to work on our delivery. A sermon is only as good as it is delivered. Our sermons may have great information, but if our presentation is ineffective all that information is wasted.

As you prepare and rehearse your sermons, here are four things to work on to help you deliver your messages effectively:

1. **Control your power.**

   By *power* I mean the volume of your voice. Some preachers don't have any problems with being heard. You may be one of them. You may project your voice well and present your sermons with confidence. That's a good thing! However, be careful not to overwhelm your listeners with high volume. If you preach your entire sermon at a high level of volume, your listeners will likely tune you out or you might come across as angry instead of passionate.

   Make your volume work for you. As with a good song, there is a time to turn down the volume and a time to turn it up for optimum effect. The content and movement of your sermon should help you determine your volume level. Don't be like the preacher who wrote these words in his sermon notes: "Sermon weak here, get louder." Your volume should reflect the tone of your content.

   Establish a medium-volume level for your introduction and transitions. Be sure it is comfortable for you and your listeners. Next, determine a low-volume level for touching or dramatic moments in your sermon (but be sure you can still be heard!). Finally, establish a high-volume level for those convicted and passionate sections of your sermon. Always be mindful of those three volume levels and your sermon delivery will improve immensely.

2. **Vary your pace.**

   Speed may kill on the highway but talking too slow will kill a sermon. If you are a slow speaker most of your listeners are probably checked out. The human mind thinks much faster than it hears. If listeners have to slow down their thinking to listen to you they will get bored quickly.

Speaking at a comfortably swift pace not only helps your listeners track your sermon better, but also conveys excitement and energy. Listen to some of your favorite preachers and I bet you will find that they speak at a reasonably quick pace.

Preaching at a quicker pace also makes the moments when you slow down that much more effective. Just like your volume, there are moments when you need to vary your pace of speech. Once again, your content should determine when you need to slow down or speed up.

You can speak too quickly, and if you have that tendency, work on slowing down. However, I have learned that most preachers don't have that problem. It's time to pick up the pace! Your listeners will thank you.

3. **Fluctuate your pitch.**

Remember the teacher in the movie *Ferris Bueller's Day Off* who called roll in a monotone voice, "Bueller, Bueller?" Don't be that person in the pulpit. There is nothing worse than when preachers fail to vary their pitch and voice inflections. Sometimes it can be hypnotic and put you right to sleep.

Varying your pitch is what gives your sermons personality. Of course, don't be robotic about it. Your voice inflections should be natural. In fact, your mind already knows how to vary the pitch of your voice based on words and feelings. The trick is letting go of control and allowing your mind and mouth to work as they should.

If you struggle with varying your pitch, pay attention to how you speak in conversations with friends. You might want to record yourself (get permission from your friends!). Feel that state you are in when you speak naturally with friends and work to replicate it in the pulpit.

4. **Remember to pause.**

   The pause is the most underrated aspect of sermon delivery. When used well a pause can dramatically affect the way your message comes across. A well-timed pause can work wonders in a sermon. It also gives your listeners a time to catch their breath or reflect on something important you said. A good way to work on pausing is to read poetry out loud. This will help you develop timing and rhythm as you speak.

   Pausing also helps eliminate fillers like "um," "you know," and "like." A filler here and there is not an issue, but if you find yourself adding them regularly try replacing them with a pause. You will be amazed how much sharper you will sound.

HOW TO PREACH WITHOUT NOTES

Understanding and practicing the proper mechanics of delivery is important, but to be an eventful preacher you must also learn to preach without being tied to your notes. Preparing notes or a manuscript can be an effective practice for preachers, but being stuck to them while you preach is fatal. It takes a very special preacher to read a sermon effectively in the pulpit. For the rest of us it is virtually impossible to engage and inspire our listeners if our noses are buried in our notes. Find a way to preach without being tied to your notes or script and listeners will thank you.

So, what's the secret to preaching without notes? Preachers use different techniques and approaches. Here are four approaches to move away from referencing notes that I have found helpful:

1. **Start preparing early in the week.**

   Sometimes the demands of ministry will require starting sermon preparation later in the week but making a habit of it will diminish your effectiveness and ability to remember sermons. Preparing early gives your mind the time to marinate on your message and make key changes, additions or adjustments. It will also give time for your brain to memorize and internalize the message. When you get up to preach you will feel confident and sharp without a need to constantly look down at your notes. A restaurant that serves my favorite steak marinates it in juices for a week. That is why it tastes so good. Good sermons are the same way. They take time to develop and it takes your brain time to absorb them so you can preach with freedom and confidence.

2. **Construct a "memory palace."**

   One effective technique many preachers and other communicators use to present without being tied to notes is called a "Memory Palace."[2] It is quite simple. You break down your sermon into small parts and then associate each part with a room or object in your house. As you preach your sermon you visualize walking through your house touching the objects or entering the rooms you associate with each part of your sermon. The best way to utilize this approach is to visualize a routine you have in your home. Perhaps it is how you normally come into the house when returning home from work or how you move about your house when getting up in the morning. Prepare the sequence of your sermon to follow the sequence of that routine. For example: bathroom/shower is a story about a powerful baptism; a coffee maker and cup is your scripture text about being renewed ("Look! I'm doing a new thing" [Isa 43:19 NRSV]); your closet is how God's work of renewal affects your outward appearance and behavior, and so on.

3. **Identify and use mind-triggering words.**

   Many preachers find it difficult to remember the sequence of their sermon and how one movement of thought is tied to the next. A technique that can be useful in aiding memory is placing a word or transition phrase at the end of each section that will trigger your memory of the next section. For example, the last sentence of your introduction may be "I have often wondered why bad things happen to *good people*. . . ." The words *good people* will trigger your next movement of thought, which begins with this story or illustration: "I remember a good person in my life who was tragically killed. . . ."

4. **Understand your sermon's movement.**

   This may seem painfully obvious, but perhaps the best advice to preaching without being tied to notes is to understand your sermon. Preaching guru Tom Long emphasizes the need to "understand what you are going to say."[3] To understand your sermon means to know in your heart what you are trying to express. Understand the ultimate message behind all of the words. Know the essence of each section of your sermon. This way, if you forget something, it won't matter. You will know the heart of your sermon and the right words will come to you.

As I conclude this chapter, I want to reemphasize that the practice of rigorously rehearsing sermons is what separates great preachers from the rest. So, go practice your sermon!

Conclusion
SIGNS OF SERMON SUCCESS

How do you know if your sermon is successful? The feedback you receive from listeners can be helpful. Look for the following responses from your listeners as indicators your sermon has connected with your congregation or other audience.[1]

1. **Your listeners remember the message.**

   One way to know if your sermons are effective is if they stick with your listeners. Do you think your listeners could repeat the point (or points) of your sermons at lunch after worship?

   Application: Work on a "sticky statement" to repeat in your sermon that summarizes your message.

2. **Your listeners go home and read the Bible**.

   You would be hard pressed to find a better way to tell if your sermons are making an impact than if your listeners are motivated to read more of the Bible. We all want our listeners to grow in their understanding of God's word. If a sermon compels them to take a deeper look at scripture, well done!

Application: Provide room in your sermon to break down and explain your scripture text.

3. **Your listeners set up an appointment with you.**

   Quite often a good litmus test for sermon effectiveness is the number of phone calls you receive from listeners who want to come in and talk to you. Good preaching should provoke people to grow.

   Application: Be sure your sermons are addressing relevant topics and struggles of your listeners.

4. **Your listeners act on the message.**

   This one may seem obvious but it is a good reminder that good preachers always ask, "What do I want my listeners to do with my sermon?" Every sermon needs a handle on it. Otherwise it will be left in the sanctuary.

   Application: As you prepare sermons always ask, "How can listeners apply this message to their lives?"

5. **Your listeners make a profession of faith in Christ.**

   You can't make a list like this without including one of our primary goals as preachers—that is, to proclaim the gospel and make disciples of Jesus Christ. One of the greatest feelings in the world is knowing that your sermon, by the power of the Holy Spirit, moved people to surrender their lives to Christ. Fellow preachers, that's what it's all about.

   Application: Don't forget to preach sermons that call people to a relationship with Jesus Christ!

6. **Your listeners want to join the church.**

   Let's be honest. Christians don't grow unless they are rooted in a local church. If a sermon motivates them to make a commitment to your church, then praise God!

   Application: Preach a handful sermons each year that address the importance of being active in the church and rooted in the body of Christ. Oh, don't forget to mention tithing!

7. **Your listeners talk about the sermon with other people.**

   A tried and true way to increase worship attendance is to preach sermons that motivate your listeners to talk to other people about your church. Word of mouth is still the best way to grow a church.

   Application: Share your best sermons on social media.

8. **Your listeners send you angry letters and email.**

   If you are faithful to the preaching task, there will be times when you are led to preach messages that are not popular with listeners. If your listeners are always agreeing with you, check to see if you are challenging them enough.

   Application: Don't forget to be prophetic in your preaching by addressing moral and social concerns.

INTERLUDE

PROVIDE A SERMON TRANSCRIPT

In my twenty-plus years of preaching I have learned that there are few things more valuable to my preaching ministry than providing transcripts of my sermons. Here are five good reasons you should provide a sermon transcript:

1. Some people would rather read a sermon than watch it.

Although sermon podcasts and videos are helpful, a sermon transcript is far from obsolete. Those unable to attend worship often find it easier and more convenient to read a sermon instead of watching it on their computer or mobile device. Some people like to read over a sermon after they have heard it to reinforce their learning or find something they missed. A sermon transcript can also be a real Godsend to those who are hearing impaired.

2. Your sermons will reach more people.

I once received a letter from someone who lives twelve hundred miles away who looks forward to receiving my sermon manuscripts in the mail each week. She stated they have been a source of comfort and strength. This is just one letter among many. I have received several letters and email from prisoners and shut-ins to folks who saw one of my transcripts in the waiting room of a doctor's office in another state! It is amazing the journeys your sermons will take as transcripts. They will wind up in the hands of people you did not expect and transform them in surprising ways.

3. You have a record of what you said–and didn't say!

Every preacher knows what it's like to be misquoted. If you have a transcript of what you said, you can clear up matters rather quickly. What's more is that if the news media wants to do a story on you or your church they usually want good quotes. You will have a large source of material to draw from.

4. You can have your sermons published.

Your discipline of providing weekly transcripts of sermons can pay off in the form of a published book. You've done all the writing. All there is left to do is some editing. I know some preachers who have published e-books of sermons on websites like Amazon. Publishing a book of sermons is a great way to spread the good news and help other preachers who are looking for sermon ideas and illustrations.

5. Your sermons will find a second life in your church.

I have discovered that providing sermon transcripts for my congregation gives my sermons a second life. Small groups and Bible studies use them as curriculum. I have added discussion questions to some of my sermons, which make them very user friendly for group study. We also publish sermons on our website and post excerpts of sermons on social media. This creates more discussion and conversation.

Obviously, manuscript preachers will find it easier to provide a sermon transcript. However, even if you preach from notes or an outline, there are plenty of resources available that can transcribe your sermon recording.

Afterword
THE BIG TEN

Ten Things Great Preachers Do Differently

The seed of this book was my search for what great preachers do differently. In my search for preaching excellence, I often ask: *What separates good preachers from great preachers?* Many think it is skill or talent. While I wouldn't argue that some of the great preachers you admire are gifted communicators, great talent is not essential to be a great preacher. I invite you to learn and apply what great preachers do differently.

TEN THINGS GREAT PREACHERS DO DIFFERENTLY[1]

Far from exhaustive, here is my "Big Ten" list of what great preachers do differently:

1. **Connect with listeners.**

   If people don't connect with you, they will not listen to you. If people won't listen to you, they will not hear your message. If people don't hear your message, you're wasting your time.

Great preachers know that in order to get their messages across they must connect with listeners. How do they do this? By preparing messages with their listeners' perspective in mind, not their own. Most of your listeners have not been to seminary. They don't care about the great theologians or the Greek words of the New Testament. What they care about is if the message you are preaching will make a difference to their lives. Now before you say something about giving itching ears what they want to hear (2 Tim 4:3), know that connecting with listeners doesn't mean sacrificing the substance of your sermons. You can still preach rich, biblical, and challenging sermons, but in order for those sermons to be heard you must frame them in a way that is interesting to your listeners. What questions are your listeners asking? Why should they care about your sermon?

2. **Preach with conviction.**

   Great preachers study a scripture text to find a sermon they need to hear and then preach that sermon to their listeners. This ensures that the sermon will be preached with genuine passion and conviction. Great preachers feel they will die unless they communicate what God has put on their hearts to say. Once again, conviction is the secret sauce of great preaching because a convicted preacher is a compelling preacher.

3. **Preach for response.**

   Great preachers are always asking, "What do I want my listeners to *do* with my sermon?" A lot of sermons contain the *what, who, when, where,* and *why*. Very few sermons contain the *how*. Great preachers are always moving from inspiration to application. They are always thinking about how their ideas and points can be applied in relevant and concrete ways. Great preachers also know that the gospel demands a response. They give listeners the opportunity to respond to their messages through responding to an old-fashioned altar call, repeating a prayer at their seat, putting a pledge card on the altar, or some practical application of the sermon during the week. Sermons should not be left in the sanctuary. Don't just say it, show it!

4. **Open the scriptures.**

   Great preachers make scripture come alive for their listeners. They bring out the wisdom and life changing truth in God's word. They make the Bible relatable and easy to understand. Great preachers motivate listeners to go home and read their Bible. If listeners tell you they went home after worship and read their Bible, you have succeeded, my friend.

5. **Communicate authentically.**

   Great preachers have found their voice. They realize that God wants to use their unique personalities to communicate the gospel. Phillips Brooks defined preaching as "truth through personality." It is OK to learn from other preachers and even emulate some of their qualities, but you will never become a great preacher trying to be someone you are not. Besides, today's listeners can smell an inauthentic preacher from a mile away. God has called *you* to preach the gospel. Great preachers are not afraid to be themselves in the pulpit.

6. **Cultivate a deep spiritual life.**

I once heard someone say that congregations never rise above the spiritual maturity of their leaders. I believe this with all my heart. Great preaching comes from the fruit of your relationship with God. If you are always seeking to grow in your faith, you will never run out of sermon material. Congregations cannot thrive without feeding on nutritious spiritual meals and pastors cannot survive ministry without proper spiritual nutrition.

7. **Build a big tool box.**

   Great preachers are always on the prowl for sermon material and illustrations and develop the discipline of writing them down and filing them away. There are many ways to do this. Write small topic notes in the table of contents of books, type in ideas in the "notes" app of your phone, keep a small notebook in your pocket at all times, create a box for sermon material and illustrations and throw copies of articles and notes in it, or keep a legal pad and pen on your desk and on your bedside table. Great preachers keep filling the well.

8. **Preach from brokenness.**

   Great preachers are not afraid to be vulnerable. This does not mean using the pulpit and your congregation as a therapist and airing all of your dirty laundry. However, profound healing can occur in your listeners when you are willing to share out of your brokenness. In fact, it could be said that you really don't start preaching until you have been broken and experience God in your brokenness. What you learn in the midst of your valleys will make up some of your best sermons.

9. **Rehearse.**

   Once again, what separates great preachers from the rest is the discipline of rehearsing sermons. Great preachers always rehearse their sermons before they preach them. They truly know their sermons "by heart." Whether you prepare a manuscript, an oral manuscript, or an outline, if you want to go from good to great as a preacher, rehearse your sermons. Your praise band rehearses. Your choir rehearses. Why should we as preachers be exempt from rehearsing? And don't think that rehearsing will prevent your sermons from sounding lively and fresh. The opposite is true. Rehearsing your sermons will give you more freedom in the pulpit because you will never feel lost or afraid of forgetting your ideas. There will be a well-worn sermon path in your brain that will allow you to deviate from the path when led and still find your way back home.

10. **Listen to other preachers.**

    Gone is the excuse that we as preachers can never listen to other preachers because we are always preaching. The internet contains millions of sermon videos from great preachers. Carve out time to watch them and learn from them. Observe and study what they do effectively. There will always be something you can learn and apply to your preaching ministry.

Appendix 1

FOUR WAYS YOUR PREACHING CAN BOOST WORSHIP ATTENDANCE

Pastors will disagree on just about anything except their common desire to grow a church. Even the humblest of pastors secretly wants to see more people in worship. And what's wrong with that? More people in worship means more people hearing the gospel. While reading books and attending church-growth conferences are helpful, there are some things you can do immediately that will help grow your church and it won't cost you a nickel. Here are four preaching strategies that will grow your church:[1]

1. **Do a provocative sermon series.**

   Have you ever done a provocative sermon series, that addressed homosexuality, evolution, the death penalty, biblical inerrancy, or some other hot topic? Aggressively promote such a series (especially at Christmas and Easter) and I can almost guarantee you will see an increase in worship attendance at your church.

2. **Cut back on the lectionary and preach more topical sermons.**

   Yes, following the lectionary has its benefits but I don't know of a growing and thriving church that is led by a pure lectionary preacher. I am sure there are exceptions but I don't know of any. Most listeners are drawn to sermons that address relevant topics. Many of your listeners are not dying to hear what the Bible has to say. You have to work harder than that. Create a desire in listeners to hear what the Bible has to say about a topic they care about and then they will want to know more about the Bible. You don't have to give up the lectionary but expand your preaching ministry by being topical from time to time.

3. **Do a "You Asked for It" series and poll your congregation for sermon topics.**

   Use your sermon time to answer questions from the congregation. Early in the service ask them to write down a question and put it in the offering plate. During the offertory or another praise song pick out the ones you want to answer and then read and answer them during your sermon time. Also poll your church for what subject they would like a sermon to address and then put a "You Asked for It" series together based on their responses.

4. **Post your sermons on Facebook.**

   When you preach a sermon that really resonates with people, be sure to post the video on Facebook and encourage people to comment and share. You may also want to try posting a quote or paragraph of your sermon on Facebook and ask people to respond and share. If your church doesn't have a Facebook page, get one! Today, a Facebook page is just as important as a website.

Appendix 2

SHOW ME THE MONEY

Nothing strikes fear in the hearts of most pastors than the idea of preaching about money. I know preachers who never preach about stewardship and leave it to the laity to discuss. Those same pastors often complain why giving is so low and pledges aren't coming in. It's not rocket science.

Pastors who preach about tithing and giving are more likely to have financially healthy churches. Stewardship, like every other important initiative in the church, must be led from the top. Why would a congregation feel compelled to give, if giving is never mentioned from the pulpit? The pulpit is the engine that drives the train of the church. If a preacher never talks about tithing it communicates that faithful giving is not a priority.

Three Questions Every Stewardship Sermon Should Answer

Let me share three vital questions a successful stewardship sermon must directly address:

1. **Why give?**

   Many churches are not financially healthy because they have not been taught the spiritual discipline of tithing. If they've had a succession of pastors whose lips were sealed about money, then they are likely to have a generation of parishioners who don't have a clue what tithing is or why it is important. Start with why:

   Jesus said, "Where your treasure is, there your heart will be also" (Matt 6:21). We spend money on what is most important to us. Show me someone's bank statement and I will show you their priorities.

   Tithing reminds us that God is the owner of everything.

   Tithing is a spiritual discipline that helps us put God first in our lives.

2. **Why pledge?**

   You will always have folks who give but refuse to pledge. This makes finance committee meetings more frustrating than playing golf. A good stewardship sermon drives home the importance of pledging. Why pledge?

   A pledge is a sign of faithfulness and obedience to God. Your pledge is your promise to join God in working in and through the church.

   A pledge is a way of holding yourself accountable to God and the church. When you write your commitment down you are more likely to follow through with it.

   Churches must have pledges to plan a ministry budget. A church cannot plan a budget effectively without having a solid projection of giving.

3. **Why give to the church?**

   There are so many schools and nonprofits asking for money. While supporting these organizations is important, nothing should take the place of our financial commitment to the church. The church is God's best hope for the world. The church is God's chosen vessel: "Now you are the body of Christ and individually members of it" (1 Cor 12:27 NRSV). When we don't give, something God wants done does not get done.

   The late, renowned pastor Bill Self said that there are four great doctrines of the Bible: God, sin, redemption, and stewardship. Everyone wants the first three preached, but many folks are not fond of the last one. However, without proper stewardship your faith and church will never thrive.

   The famed Dallas Cowboys Football coach Tom Landry once said, "Leadership is getting someone to do what they don't want to do, to achieve what they want to achieve." That's a good description of the role of a minister, especially when preaching a sermon on financial stewardship: "Bring the full tithe into the storehouse, so that there may be food in my house, and thus put me to the test, says the Lord of hosts; see if I will not open the windows of heaven for you and pour down for you and overflowing blessing" (Mal 3:10 NRSV).

DEALING WITH COMPLAINTS

If after preaching on money people complain or send nasty email, just remember the old story about the doctor who was doing a physical examination and pressed on the abdomen of a patient.

The patient screamed, "Ouch! Why did you do that?" The doctor replied, "It shouldn't hurt there." If people complain about stewardship sermons they are simply diagnosing their own spiritual problem.

Preaching on tithing and giving is worth having to deal with a few complaints and nasty emails. You're investing in the health of your church. Besides, a mean letter is nothing compared to what Jesus experienced. Here are some tips for a successful stewardship sermon:

- Acknowledge visitors in worship: "If you are visitor with us today, I imagine you were hoping my sermon would NOT be about money! Well, you are off the hook. Please feel no obligation to pledge or give. I believe this message will convey that we are a generous church and you will want to learn more about us."
- Fill out your pledge card in front of your church and say, "I would never ask you to do something I was not willing to do." It is hard to argue with that.
- Announce the percentage of members who don't give a cent to the church. That should wake them up!
- Break down numbers: "If one hundred people gave just $20 a week we would have $100,000 of new money to spend on ministries."
- Share how much you give. Sadly, in some churches the pastor is one of the top givers. This may encourage your church to rethink their giving!
- If all else fails, use this old line, "The Bible says 'God loves a cheerful giver,' but the church will take a grumpy one!"

Appendix 3

TEN BOOKS EVERY PREACHER MUST READ

Every leader is a reader. The same goes for preachers. The effective preachers I know are constantly trying to improve their craft by reading the best books on preaching and communication. Here are ten books that offer insights I believe every preacher would be wise to consider:[1]

1. ***Resonate: Present Visual Stories That Transform Audiences*** by Nancy Duarte (Wiley, 2010).

   Nancy Duarte is a communication expert who has analyzed countless sermons and speeches in search of the holy grail for creating effective presentations. She has found it, and in this fascinating and enlightening book she reveals it. If you want the secret ingredient to preaching captivating sermons read this book.

2. ***Made to Stick: Why Some Ideas Survive and Others Die*** by Chip and Dan Heath (Random House, 2007).

   This book should be required reading for every preaching and public speaking class. It is not specifically about verbal communication, but it applies to anyone who wants their message to be remembered. There is a reason why you remember some messages and forget others. If you want your sermon to live beyond Sunday heed the advice of the Heath brothers.

3. ***Surviving the Stained-Glass Jungle*** by William L. Self (Mercer University Press, 2014).

   A pastor of large churches for over fifty years, Bill Self was a spectacular preacher and ministry sage. He passed away a few years ago, but his indispensable wisdom lives on in this invaluable book. His chapter on preaching alone is worth one hundred times the cost of the book. Read it and go from good to great as a preacher and pastor.

4. ***Communicating for a Change: Seven Keys to Irresistible Communication*** by Andy Stanley and Lane Jones (Multnomah, 2006).

   It is foolish not to learn from one of the best Christian communicators in the country. Regardless of how you may feel about Stanley's theology or approach, there is a reason why he leads one of the largest churches in America and pastors flock to Atlanta to learn from him. If you want to learn how to preach to millennials buy this book.

5. ***TED Talks: The Official TED Guide to Public Speaking*** by Chris Anderson (Mariner Books, 2016).

   The popularity of TED Talks is good news for preachers. Public speaking as a medium is very much alive and well. Of course, not all sermons are as engaging as many TED Talks, which is why every preacher should read this book. Chris Anderson is the "head cheese" of TED Talks, and in this book he lays out why so many TED Talks are compelling and shows you how to apply the principles to your sermons and presentations. Have this one nearby when you prepare sermons.

6. ***The Witness of Preaching*** by Thomas G. Long (Westminster John Knox Press, 2016).

   This is the only preaching textbook on the list. I don't have a problem with textbooks, but they are not always accessible and practical. What I like about Long's book is that it combines homiletic theory with practice. His chapter on biblical exegesis for preaching is the best one I've read on the subject. Stay sharp as a biblical preacher by reading this book.

7. ***Determining the Form: Elements of Preaching*** by O. Wesley Allen Jr. (Fortress Press, 2009).

   The importance of sermon design cannot be overstated. Remember that it is not just what a sermon is about; it's how it's about it. Allen has a strong grasp on different sermon forms and styles, and he shows you how to use them effectively in your own preaching. Read this book and you will be able to structure your sermons with power.

8. ***Moving Mountains: The Art of Letting Others See Things Your Way*** by Henry M. Boettinger (Macmillan/Collier, 1989).

   This book is out of print, but its principles are timeless. Snag a used copy off the Internet. If you only buy the book for chapter 3, "How to Get and Hold Attention," it is well worth the price. Forty years ago, Boettinger discovered the same holy grail for irresistible presentations as Nancy Duarte. In chapter 3 he dissects the "grail" and gives you a deeper understanding of the technique.

9. ***Public Speaking as Listeners Like It!*** by Richard C. Borden (Harper, 1935).

   This is by far the oldest book on the list. It has been out of print for years but do yourself a favor and find a used copy on Amazon. I know public speaking instructors who would not sell their copy for a hundred dollars. In the book, longtime public-speaking guru Richard Borden lays out his simple "Borden Formula" for giving speeches. But don't let the simplicity of his approach fool you. Try preaching your next sermon using his method and watch what happens. You will be amazed.

10. ***The Sir Winston Method: The Five Secrets of Speaking the Language of Leadership*** by James C. Humes (Quill, 1993).

    What preacher could not benefit from learning about what made Winston Churchill a great communicator? Hume is a longtime expert on public speaking, and in this intriguing book he unpacks Churchill's formula for success as an orator. This book contains priceless gems that will improve your skills as a communicator.

Preface

1. "Choosing a New Church or House of Worship," Pew Research Center, August 23, 2016, http://www.pewforum.org/2016/08/23/choosing-a-new-church-or-house-of-worship/.

2. Joshua Pease, "Gallup Research: What Keeps People Coming Back to Church Week after Week Isn't the Cool Music," April 27, 2017, https://churchleaders.com/news/302891-gallup-research-keeps-people-coming-back-church-week-week-isnt-cool-music.html.

3. Charley Reeb, *That'll Preach! 5 Simple Steps to Your Best Sermon Ever* (Nashville: Abingdon Press, 2017).

Introduction

1. Charles D. Reeb, *One Heaven of a Party* (Lima, OH: CSS Publishing, 2003), 10.

2. J. Wallace Hamilton, "Sermon Preparation" (essay, Pasadena Community Church, St. Petersburg, FL, n.d.).

Essential Element #1

1. Ken Untener, *Preaching Better: Practical Suggestions for Homilists* (New York: Paulist Press, 1999), chap. 8.

2. “Religion is reaching for God; Christianity is reaching for us” is from my sermon “Why I Follow Jesus” preached at Johns Creek UMC, July 1, 2018, and alluded to in other sermons, including “Why Christianity?” preached at Pasedena Community Church, December 24, 2017. “You know the Spirit is within you when you have power beyond you” is from my sermon “We Believe in the Holy Spirit” preached at Johns Creek UMC, Oct. 21, 2018. “Sometimes the only way to the mountain top is through the valley,” is from my sermon “A Closer Look at the Twenty-third Psalm,” preached at Pasadena Community Church, October 2011.

3. “Creating a Sticky Statement for Sermons,” Ignite Discipleship, October 8, 2013, http://ignitediscipleship.com/2013/10/08/crafting-a-sticky-statement-for-sermons/.

4. Cary Nieuwhof, “How to Craft a Killer Bottom Line for Your Next Talk,” https://careynieuwhof.com/how-to-craft-a-killer-bottom-line-for-your-next-talk/.

5. Charles D. Reeb, *One Heaven of a Party* (Lima, OH: CSS), 133.

6. Nieuwhof.

7. Ibid.

8. From Frederick Buechner’s novel *The Final Beast* (New York: Seabury Press, 1967).

9. Nieuwhof.

10. Ibid.

Essential Element #2

1. “It’s Not What a Movie Is about, It’s How It Is about It,’ Roger Ebert 1942–2013,” Pop Lifer (blog), https://poplifer

.com/2013/04/05/its-not-what-a-movie-is-about-its-how-it-is-about-it-roger-ebert-1942-2013/.

2. Jim Coyle, "Steven Pinker: 'Beware the Curse of Knowledge,'" *The Star*, November 23, 2014, https://www.thestar.com/news/insight/2014/11/23/steven_pinker_beware_the_curse_of_knowledge.html.

3. "Present Your Ideas: Overcome the 'Curse of Knowledge,'" Big Think, April 29, 2015 http://bigthink.com/big-think-edge/chris-anderson-and-how-to-overcome-the-curse-of-knowledge-to-become-a-better-presenter.

4. Richard Borden, *Public Speaking as Listeners Like It*, (New York: Harper, 1935), 3–15.

5. Ibid.

6. A. H. Monroe, *Monroe's Principles of Speech*, (Chicago: Scott, Foresman, 1943).

7. Charley Reeb, *That'll Preach! 5 Simple Steps to Your Best Sermon Ever* (Nashville: Abingdon, 2017), 66.

8. Charley Reeb, "Preaching for a Verdict: Why You Should See Your Listeners Like a Jury," Ministry Pass, July 26, 2017, https://ministrypass.com/preaching-for-a-verdict-why-you-should-see-your-listeners-like-a-jury/.

9. I am grateful to my friend Roberta Flowers for her insights.

10. Adapted from *That'll Preach!*, 76.

Interlude: Preaching to Millennials

1. Michael Duduit, "3 Tips for Preaching to Millennials," Preaching.com, https://www.preaching.com/articles/3-tips-for-preaching-to-millennials/. Reprinted with permission.

Essential Element #3

1. Reg Grant and John Reed, "Taking a Different Route: Creativity in Sermon Structure," in *The Power Sermon: Countdown to Quality Messages for Maximum Impact* (Ada, MI: Baker Books, 2013), chap. 11.

2. Adapted from *That'll Preach! 5 Simple Steps to Your Best Sermon Ever* by Charley Reeb (Nashville: Abingdon, 2017), 73.

3. Yancey Arrington, *Preaching That Moves People* (League City, TX: Clear Creek Resources, 2018), 95–103.

4. Nancy Duarte provides great insight into how effective sermons and speeches create emotional contrast (see Nancy Duarte, *Resonate: Present Visual Stories That Transform Audiences* [Sunnyvale, CA: Duarte, 2012], chap. 6, iBooks).

5. Ibid.

Interlude: Keep It Short

1. Dan Wunderlich, "A Career in Preaching—Part 1 with Bishop Ken Carter," Art of the Sermon podcast, https://artofthesermon.fireside.fm/25.

Essential Element #4

1. Akash Karia, *How to Deliver a Great TED Talk: Presentation Secrets of the World's Best Speakers* (self-pub., 2013), chap. 22, ebook.

2. See "Kurt Vonnegut on the Shapes of Stories," https://www.youtube.com/watch?v=oP3c1h8v2ZQ.

3. See "Rule of Three," https://en.wikipedia.org/wili/Rule_of_three_(writing).

4. Roy H. Williams, *The Wizard of Ads: Turning Words into Magic and Dreamers into Millionaires* (Austin: Bard Press, 1998), chap. 13, Kindle.

5. Ben Decker and Kelly Decker, *Communicate to Influence: How to Inspire Your Audience to Action* (New York: McGraw Hill, 2015), chap. 5, Kindle.

6. See the sermon by King Duncan entitled "Choices" from sermons.com, https://sermons.com/sermon/choices/1351792.

7. Hayakawa (1906–1992) published a book co-authored with Alan R. Hayakawa titled *Language in Thought and Action.* (Houghton Mifflin Harcourt, 1990).

8. Ibid, 53–54.

9. Charles D. Reeb, *One Heaven of a Party: Sermons on the First Readings for Lent and Easter Cycle C* (Lima, OH: CSS Publications, 2003), 50.

10. I am grateful to Wayne Cordeiro for using a similar illustration in his presentation at Hyde Park UMC, Tampa, Florida, February 2004.

11. Adapted from *That'll Preach!*, 28.

Essential Element #5

1. See "Loyalty beyond Reason," a September 22, 2004 blog post by Kevin Roberts that quotes Donald Calne. http://www.redrose.consulting/speeches/loyalty-beyond-reason/.

2. Michael Port, *Steal the Show* (New York: Houghton Mifflin Harcourt, 2015), chap. 11, ebook.

3. Inspired by Elton Trueblood's *The Humor of Christ* (New York: Harper & Row, 1964).

4. Akash Karia, *How to Deliver a Great TED Talk: Presentation Secrets of the World's Best Speakers* (self-pub., 2013), chap. 19, ebook.

5. Ibid.

6. Ibid.

7. Ibid.

8. Based on a sermon by Bishop Sue Haupert-Johnson at an annual conference of The United Methodist Church, Lakeland, Florida, June 7, 2018.

Interlude: Preach Like TED

1. See "How Many TED TALKS Are Watched Every Day?" by Mark Lovett, https://www.quora.com/How-many-TED-TALKS-are-watched-every-day.

2. Carmine Gallo, *Talk Like TED: The 9 Public-Speaking Secrets of the World's Top Minds* (New York: St. Martin's Press, 2014), introduction, ebook.

Essential Element #6

1. June Cohen, "What Makes a Great TED Talk," September 29, 2010, https://www.youtube.com/watch?v=RVDfWfUSBIM.

2. See Luciano Passuello, "Develop Perfect Memory with the Memory Palace Technique" on his Litemind blog, https://litemind.com/memory-palace/.

3. Carey Nieuwhof, "A 5 Step Method for Delivering a Talk without Using Notes," https://careynieuwhof.com/how-to-deliver-a-talk-without-using-notes-2/.

Conclusion: Signs of Sermon Success

1. Charley Reeb, "8 Signs Your Sermons Are Making an Impact," Ministry Pass, https://ministrypass.com/signs-sermons-making-impact/. Reprinted by permission.

Afterword: The Big Ten

1. Charley Reeb, "10 Things Great Preachers Do Differently," churchleadership.com, October 5, 2016, https://www.churchleadership.com/leading-ideas/10-things-great-preachers-do/. Reprinted with permission.

Appendix 1

1. Charley Reeb, "5 Ways to Boost Your Worship Attendance This Fall," The Rocket Company, August 11, 2017, https://therocketcompany.com/5-ways-boost-worship-attendance-fall/.

Appendix 3

1. Charley Reeb, "The 2018 Effective Preacher's Reading List," December 9, 2017. Ministry Pass, https://ministrypass.com/preachers-reading-list/. Reprinted and adapted with permission.

CPSIA information can be obtained
at www.ICGtesting.com
Printed in the USA
LVHW052339280119
605569LV00003B/3

9 781501 874390